CAUSES OF THE CIVIL WAR

CAUSES OF THE CIVIL WAR

ESCAPE FROM SLAVERY: ABOLITIONISTS AND THE UNDERGROUND RAILROAD

RECONSTRUCTION AND ITS AFTERMATH: FREED SLAVES AFTER THE CIVIL WAR

SLAVE LIFE ON A SOUTHERN PLANTATION

SLAVE REVOLTS AND REBELLIONS

THE SLAVE TRADE IN COLONIAL AMERICA

WOMEN AND CHILDREN IN SLAVERY

Rare Glimpses of Slave Life

Causes of the Civil War

JENNIFER L. ROWAN

MASON CREST

PHILADELPHIA | MIAMI

MASON CREST
450 Parkway Drive, Suite D, Broomall, Pennsylvania 19008
(866) MCP-BOOK (toll-free) • www.masoncrest.com

© 2020 by Mason Crest, an imprint of National Highlights, Inc.

All rights reserved. No part of this publication may be reproduced or transmitted in any form or by any means, electronic or mechanical, including photocopying, recording, taping, or any information storage and retrieval system, without permission from the publisher.

Printed and bound in the United States of America.

CPSIA Compliance Information: Batch #RGSL2019.
For further information, contact Mason Crest at 1-866-MCP-Book.

First printing
1 3 5 7 9 8 6 4 2

ISBN (hardback) 978-1-4222-4403-6
ISBN (series) 978-1-4222-4402-9
ISBN (ebook) 978-1-4222-7418-7

Library of Congress Cataloging-in-Publication Data
on file at the Library of Congress.

Interior and cover design: Torque Advertising + Design
Production: Michelle Luke

Publisher's Note: Websites listed in this book were active at the time of publication. The publisher is not responsible for websites that have changed their address or discontinued operation since the date of publication. The publisher reviews and updates the websites each time the book is reprinted.

QR CODES AND LINKS TO THIRD-PARTY CONTENT

You may gain access to certain third-party content ("Third-Party Sites") by scanning and using the QR Codes that appear in this publication (the "QR Codes"). We do not operate or control in any respect any information, products, or services on such Third-Party Sites linked to by us via the QR Codes included in this publication, and we assume no responsibility for any materials you may access using the QR Codes. Your use of the QR Codes may be subject to terms, limitations, or restrictions set forth in the applicable terms of use or otherwise established by the owners of the Third-Party Sites. Our linking to such Third-Party Sites via the QR Codes does not imply an endorsement or sponsorship of such Third-Party Sites or the information, products, or services offered on or through the Third-Party Sites, nor does it imply an endorsement or sponsorship of this publication by the owners of such Third-Party Sites.

TABLE OF CONTENTS

Chapter 1: Seeds of Discord.. 7
Chapter 2: Conflict and Compromise 19
Chapter 3: A Deepening Divide 29
Chapter 4: From Bleeding Kansas to Harper's Ferry ... 39
Chapter 5: The Election of 1860 & Secession Winter .. 49
Chapter 6: "Let Us Die to Make Men Free" 59
Series Glossary of Key Terms.. 70
Chapter Notes... 72
Further Reading 74
Internet Resources 75
Chronology... 76
Index 78
Author's Biography and Credits 80

KEY ICONS TO LOOK FOR:

Words to Understand: These words with their easy-to-understand definitions will increase the reader's understanding of the text while building vocabulary skills.

Sidebars: This boxed material within the main text allows readers to build knowledge, gain insights, explore possibilities, and broaden their perspectives by weaving together additional information to provide realistic and holistic perspectives.

Educational videos: Readers can view videos by scanning our QR codes, providing them with additional educational content to supplement the text. Examples include news coverage, moments in history, speeches, iconic sports moments, and much more!

Text-Dependent Questions: These questions send the reader back to the text for more careful attention to the evidence presented there.

Research Projects: Readers are pointed toward areas of further inquiry connected to each chapter. Suggestions are provided for projects that encourage deeper research and analysis.

Series Glossary of Key Terms: This back-of-the-book glossary contains terminology used throughout this series. Words found here increase the reader's ability to read and comprehend higher-level books and articles in this field.

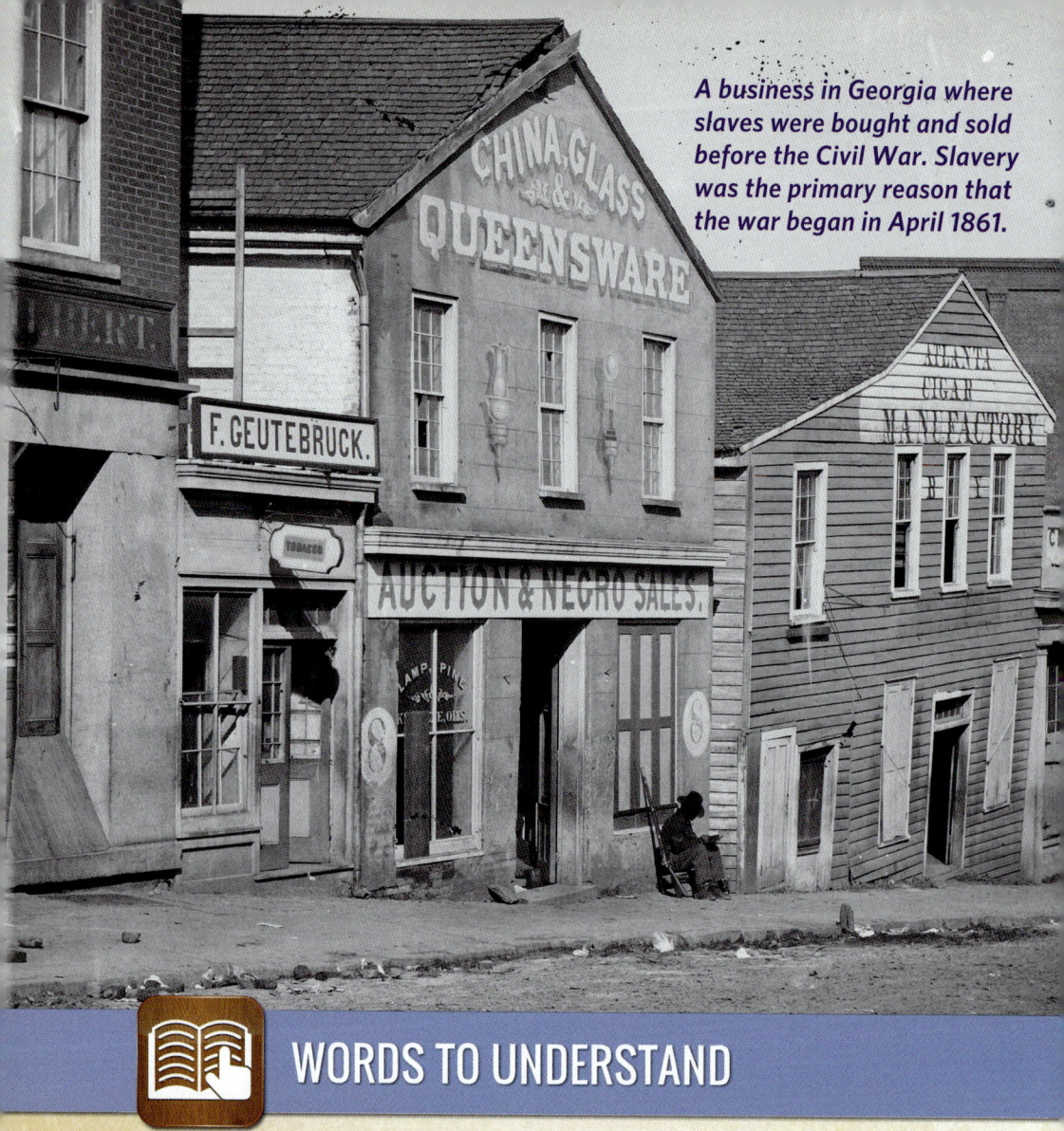

A business in Georgia where slaves were bought and sold before the Civil War. Slavery was the primary reason that the war began in April 1861.

WORDS TO UNDERSTAND

To **apportion** is to divide and assign something, such as the allocation of resources or people.

The **Articles of Confederation** was the first written constitution of the United States, ratified in 1781 to establish a central Congress to represent the 13 states in issues affecting the country as a whole.

A **bicameral legislature** consists of two houses or chambers, usually with one house holding more power of governance than the other.

CHAPTER 1

Seeds of Discord

In an 1820 letter explaining his position on the expansion of slavery into Missouri, Thomas Jefferson described the institution of slavery as having "the wolf by the ear, and we can neither hold him, nor safely let him go."

Jefferson embodied the dichotomy of early America's identity when it came to enslaving Africans and African Americans. He was a man who benefited personally from the institution while promoting the ideals of freedom and equality. Indeed, the very founding of the United States was rife with conflict when it came to the issue of slavery.

By the time of the constitution's ratification in 1787, slavery was inextricably embedded in the economy and social structures of the time. It shaped the political landscape and, over time, pitted Americans against each other as states and regions identified as free or slave. The close of the nineteenth century's first half saw the country's boiling point, with the threat and eventual outbreak of civil war the result of decades of simmering tension over ideologies and failed compromises.

SLAVERY IN AMERICA

The system of chattel slavery came to the Americas shortly after the arrival of Europeans and the establishment of permanent colonies. The Spanish and Portuguese, having failed to enslave the indigenous populations of the Caribbean and Central and South America, turned to Africa as a source for the labor required to grow valuable cash crops that would bring wealth to the mother country.

As colonies sprang up in North America, Spain, France, and England all played a role in the expansion of slavery into lands that would one day become the United States. The system was legal in all thirteen British colonies on the eve of the American Revolution, and by 1775, when the war for independence erupted, an estimated 500,000 slaves of African origin or descent lived in the colonies. From Virginia to Georgia, where the agrarian economy flourished and the plantation system brought wealth and power to white slaveholders. New York City also boasted a high concentration of slaves, similar to that of Charleston, South Carolina.

The exploitation of enslaved Africans resulted in brutal treatment, both physically and mentally, to maintain total control over the slave population. Slavers sought to dehumanize those they held in bondage, severing family ties for the sake of profit and

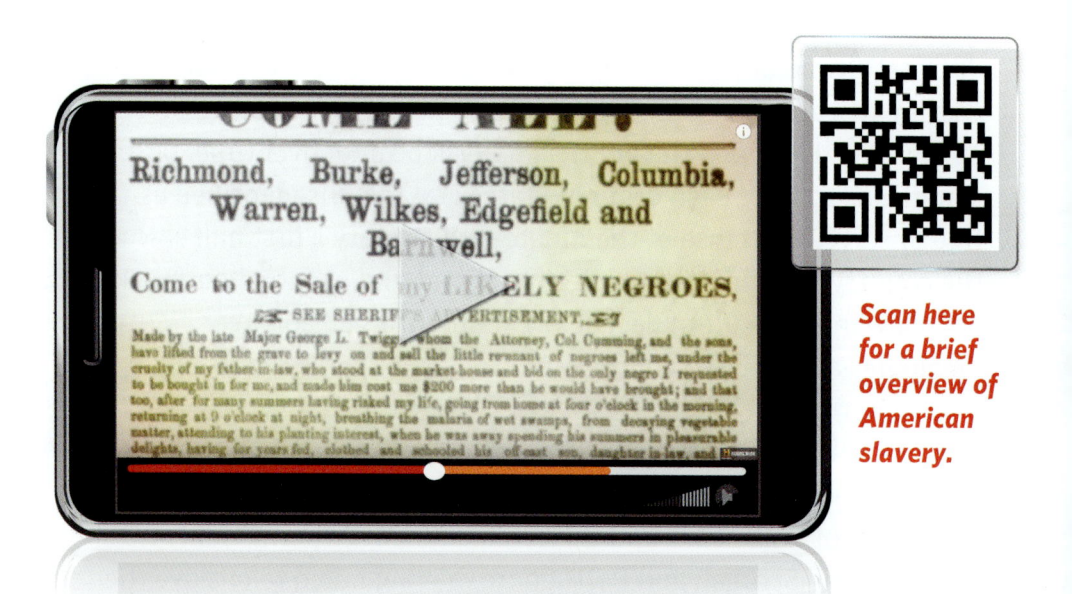

Scan here for a brief overview of American slavery.

viewing slaves not as people, but property to be bought, sold, and treated as they wished.

EARLY OPPONENTS TO SLAVERY

Opposition to slavery, while not organized into the abolitionist movement that would build in the decades just prior to the Civil War, existed in the colonies prior to the American Revolution. Enlightenment beliefs about the natural rights of life, liberty, and property drove the movement for independence. Yet how could a country be founded on freedom and democracy while also allowing slavery to exist?

Pre-revolutionary sentiment against slavery initially came from moral and religious grounds. Soon, arguments would cite economic, political, and cultural repercussions to the continuation of slavery and the slave trade in addition to moral objections. Further, as colonists used Enlightenment philosophies to justify their wish to break ties with Great Britain, opponents of slavery used the same philosophies to enumerate the rights of slaves as they corresponded with the rights of colonists.

Religious leaders and communities made up the core of American slavery's earliest

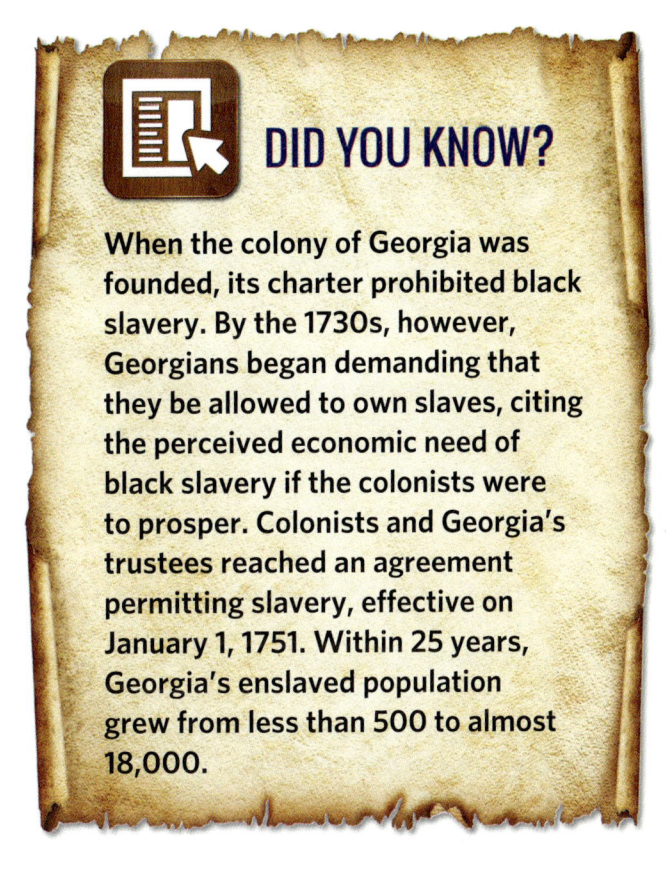

DID YOU KNOW?

When the colony of Georgia was founded, its charter prohibited black slavery. By the 1730s, however, Georgians began demanding that they be allowed to own slaves, citing the perceived economic need of black slavery if the colonists were to prosper. Colonists and Georgia's trustees reached an agreement permitting slavery, effective on January 1, 1751. Within 25 years, Georgia's enslaved population grew from less than 500 to almost 18,000.

vocal opponents. Quaker radicals, such as Benjamin Lay and John Woolman, spoke out against the Quakers' involvement in slavery using various methods of persuasion; by 1787, many northern Quakers had freed their slaves. Other religious leaders worked toward the liberation of slaves, as well as supported the education of blacks. Benjamin Rush published pamphlets urging Pennsylvania to end its involvement in the slave trade, which its Assembly did in 1773.

Other prominent Americans, including Abigail Adams, spoke out against slavery's hypocrisy in denying freedom to a whole race of people while fighting to gain freedom for another. Thomas Paine, famed author of the revolutionary pamphlet *Common Sense*, published an essay in 1775 that decried patriots complaints over "attempts to enslave them, while they hold so many hundred thousand in slavery." Paine became a founding member of America's first anti-slavery society, which formed in Philadelphia in April 1775.

The enslaved were not without a voice in this opposition. Phillis Wheatly, upon gaining her freedom, published a book of poems that included, among other topics, a commentary on the immorality of slavery. She became a vocal supporter of abolitionism. Enslaved blacks in Massachusetts staged protests and petitioned the colonial governor for the right to work for themselves once a week, thus earning money toward buying their own freedom. Uprisings, too, occurred throughout the colonies, as slaves attempted to win freedom for themselves by force.

Opposite page: Slavery was an accepted way of life in colonial America, and almost all of our country's Founding Fathers owned slaves. At one time Benjamin Franklin owned two slaves. As he grew older, his views on slavery changed and he freed his slaves. Toward the end of his life, Franklin joined the Pennsylvania Society for Promoting the Abolition of Slavery, an early abolitionist group. Franklin wrote this letter in 1789, asking that the federal government end slavery and educate former slaves so that they could become useful members of American society.

An Address
To the Public,

FROM THE

Pennsylvania Society for promoting the Abolition of Slavery, and the Relief of Free Negroes, unlawfully held in Bondage.

It is with peculiar satisfaction we assure the friends of humanity, that in prosecuting the design of our association, our endeavours have proved successful, far beyond our most sanguine expectations.

Encouraged by this success, and by the daily progress of that luminous and benign spirit of liberty, which is diffusing itself throughout the world; and humbly hoping for the continuance of the divine blessing on our labors, we have ventured to make an important addition to our original plan, and do therefore, earnestly solicit the support and assistance, of all who can feel the tender emotions of sympathy and compassion, or relish the exalted pleasure of beneficence.

Slavery is such an atrocious debasement of human nature, that its very extirpation, if not performed with solicitous care, may sometimes open a source of serious evils.

The unhappy man who has long been treated as a brute animal, too frequently sinks beneath the common standard of the human species. The galling chains that bind his body, do also fetter his intellectual faculties, and impair the social affections of his heart. Accustomed to move like a mere machine, by the will of a master, reflection is suspended; he has not the power of choice; and reason and conscience, have but little influence over his conduct: because he is chiefly governed by the passion of fear. He is poor and friendless——perhaps worn out by extreme labor, age and disease.

Under such circumstances, freedom may often prove a misfortune to himself, and prejudicial to society.

Attention to emancipated black people, it is therefore to be hoped, will become a branch of our national police; but as far as we contribute to promote this emancipation, so far that attention is evidently a serious duty, incumbent on us, and which we mean to discharge to the best of our judgment and abilities.

To instruct; to advise; to qualify those who have been restored to freedom, for the exercise and enjoyment of civil liberty. To promote in them habits of industry; to furnish them with employments suited to their age, sex, talents, and other circumstances; and to procure their children an education calculated for their future situation in life. These are the great outlines of the annexed plan, which we have adopted, and which we conceive will essentially promote the public good, and the happiness of these our hitherto too much neglected fellow creatures.

A Plan so extensive cannot be carried into execution, without considerable pecuniary resources, beyond the present ordinary funds of the society. We hope much from the generosity of enlightened and benevolent freemen, and will gratefully receive any donations or subscriptions for this purpose, which may be made to our treasurer, James Starr, *or to* James Pemberton, *chairman, of our committee of correspondence.*

Signed by order of the Society,

B. FRANKLIN, *President.*

Philadelphia, 9th of *November,* 1789.

THE FOUNDERS DEBATE

The question of how to handle slavery in America reared its head after the American Revolution, when the Founders faced the failures of the **Articles of Confederation** and set out to write a new constitution. Slavery had not been mentioned in the Declaration of Independence, though Thomas Jefferson condemned participation in the trans-Atlantic slave trade as one of the many grievances against George III in his first draft of the founding document.

Jefferson was a contradiction in the matter of slavery. Like many other Founders, he considered the enslavement of Africans to be a terrible crime, but his prosperity and fortune were both inextricably linked to his ownership of black slaves. Despite this, Jefferson attempted to end slavery in Virginia through various acts of legislation, including a ban on the importation of enslaved Africans into the state. He also proposed a ban on slavery in lands that would become the Northwest Territory in 1783 and put forth a plan that would provide for the gradual emancipation of slaves.

By 1787, it became clear that the Articles of Confederation were no longer viable if the United States was to stabilize

Thomas Jefferson, the third president of the United States, believed that slavery was evil—yet he profited from the labor of nearly 200 slaves.

THE NORTHWEST ORDINANCE

After the American Revolution, the new United States acquired lands from Great Britain called the Northwest Territory—frontier land west of Pennsylvania, bordered by the Ohio and Mississippi Rivers and the Great Lakes, that today are referred to as the Midwest. Various ordinances passed by Congress between 1783 and 1787 divided the lands into self-governing districts and for this territory to be surveyed and subdivided.

In 1787, Congress passed the last Northwest Ordinance, which outlined how the territory would be governed and how the various districts would be admitted as states into the union. The ordinance established a population threshold of 60,000 residents for an individual territory to gain statehood, while also guaranteeing civil liberties, providing for education, and promising decent treatment to Native Americans.

The Northwest Ordinance of 1787 also outlawed slavery from the lands of the Northwest Territory. Consent for the ordinance's passage had to be unanimous, and while the establishment of new, permanently free states would have offset the overall balance of free and slave states, multiple factors allowed slave states to, in relative comfort, vote to pass the ordinance. First, the concern over the balance of free and slave states had not taken hold as strongly as it would in the early decades of the nineteenth century, especially since Kentucky and Tennessee had already been admitted as states where slavery was allowed.

Economic factors played into the ordinance's unanimous passage as well. The major cash crop grown in most plantations was tobacco, a crop that required slave labor to be profitable. Keeping slavery out of the Northwest Territory protected southern tobacco planters from competition that would eat into their profits from the tobacco market.

George Washington presides over the 1787 Constitutional Convention in Philadelphia. The adopted draft of the Constitution largely avoided dealing with the problem of slavery.

politically and economically. When the Constitutional Convention convened in Philadelphia through the summer of that year, delegates from across the states wrestled to develop a system of government that would best serve the growing nation. Their first major challenge lay in determining the form of the legislative branch and how the American people would be represented therein. The Great Compromise combined two proposed plans, one calling for equal representation for all states and the other stipulating representation in Congress based on the population of each state. But another challenge loomed that would, for decades, allow discord to grow.

THE THREE-FIFTHS COMPROMISE

The Great Compromise succeeded in creating a **bicameral legislature**, with the Senate having equal representation for all states and the House of Representatives' seats based on the population of each state. Now, a new argument arose as the framers of the Constitution attempted to define how population would be calculated.

Delegates from states with large slave populations, like Virginia and South Carolina, wanted slaves to be counted in the total population for the purpose of representation in Congress. Delegates from states with low numbers of slaves or who believed slavery itself should be rendered illegal through the Constitution, argued that slaves should not be included when determining representation since they were not considered people, but rather property. The debate held the possibility of scuttling the Constitutional Convention if enough slaveholding states refused to ratify the document without the inclusion of the enslaved population in the count for representation.

In the end, the delegates reached an uneasy and imperfect compromise. The so-called Three-Fifths Compromise appeared in Article I Section 2 of the Constitution and stated that

> Representatives and direct Taxes shall be apportioned among the several States which may be included within this Union, according to their respective Numbers, which shall be determined by adding to the whole Number of free Persons, including those bound to Service for a Term of Years, and excluding Indians not taxed, three fifths of all other Persons.

DID YOU KNOW?

By 1787, ten states had outlawed the international slave trade; only North Carolina, South Carolina, and Georgia still permitted it. But those states insisted that they would leave the Constitutional Convention if the slave trade was banned. A compromise was reached: under the Constitution, the federal government would not be able to ban the international slave trade until 1808.

When the Constitution was ratified, the Founding Fathers believed that slavery would eventually die out in the United States. It had already proven unprofitable in the northern states, which were gradually banning slavery. However, the invention of the cotton gin in 1793 created a new demand for laborers to cultivate cotton on large plantations in the Deep South. This resulted in slavery being maintained in the southern states.

Essentially, the Three-Fifths Compromise allowed for three of every five slaves to count toward a state's population in order to **apportion** representation in the House.

This clause provided slave states with greater leverage in the House of Representatives and thus more influence on legislation and the maneuvers of politics that would shape the growing nation. Since representation in the Senate was equal for all states, proponents of slavery believed that, in order to protect the institution they believed was necessary for economic stability and the preservation of the social order, slavery must be allowed to spread into new territories as Americans moved west.

TEXT-DEPENDENT QUESTIONS

1. Why were Africans first brought to the Americas as slaves?
2. On what grounds did people begin to speak out against slavery in the colonial era?
3. How did the Northwest Ordinance affect the dynamic between free and slave states?

RESEARCH PROJECT

Choose one colony from each of the three British colonial regions (New England, Middle, and Southern). Then:

1. Research the demographic trends of the enslaved population in each colony from its founding to 1775. Prepare a visual to illustrate how the population of slaves compared in each colony.
2. Research the economic, social, and political factors that contributed to the rise and (if applicable) fall of the numbers of slaves in each colony. Write a two-page essay that analyzes your findings and evaluates what you believe is the most important factor that affected slavery in each region.

Slaves work in a cotton field in Georgia.

WORDS TO UNDERSTAND

The **encomienda system** in the Spanish colonies of the New World rigidly divided society into distinct classes: peninsuláres (Spanish-born settlers in the New World), creoles (American-born of Spanish descent), mestizos (people of mixed Spanish and indigenous descent), mulattos (people of mixed Spanish and African descent), indigenous peoples, and slaves of African descent.

In the years prior to the Civil War, **sectionalism** developed in which one's loyalty was to a particular part of the nation, rather than to the nation as a whole, typically in terms of North or South, free states or slave states.

Subjugation is the action of bringing someone under domination or control, usually by force.

Tariffs are duties or taxes that are paid on particular types of imports or exports.

CHAPTER 2

Conflict and Compromise

The Northwest Ordinance settled the fate of lands bordered by the Ohio and Mississippi Rivers in terms of slavery's expansion into the territory. Southern plantation owners who depended on slave labor to plant, tend, and harvest the cash crops that enriched them did not view the farmers of the Northwest Territory as economic competitors. Kentucky entered the Union as a slave state, as did Tennessee and the Deep South states of Alabama and Mississippi in their own time. The acquisition of Florida, too, provided space for the ever more deeply entrenched system of chattel slavery in the American South to flourish, linking fortunes and economies to its perpetuation. But as the United States continued its westward stretch toward the Pacific, simmering arguments over the expansion of slavery and tensions created from **sectionalism** would begin to boil over.

AMERICAN TERRITORY GROWS

America's next major land acquisition came in 1803, when Thomas Jefferson sent future president James Monroe to negotiate with France's Napoleon Bonaparte for the sale of the vast Louisiana Territory. In terms of monetary value, the United States secured the better side of the deal for the United States, paying $15 million for a territory that doubled the size of the country.

The gain of almost 830,000 square miles of fertile prairie

lands and the arterial waterway of the Missouri River brought opportunity for Americans willing to go west—expansion that would also cause the devastation of multiple Amerindian tribes who were pushed off their ancestral lands by white settlers, sparking decades of war. Congress authorized the financing of the Lewis and Clark Expedition, which set out to survey and explore the Louisiana Territory and attempt to find a water route to the Pacific coast. Additionally, the purchase secured American control over the vital port of New Orleans.

Unlike the Northwest Territories, the status of slavery in the Louisiana Territory was never formally defined. Under French and Spanish control, slavery had been legal, and the institution continued in New Orleans and the region that would eventually become the state of Louisiana after the Purchase. Enterprising proslavery settlers believed it imperative to spread slavery into the newly acquired territory. They linked the continuation of the institution with both economic success and stability, as well as an ever-increasing belief in the necessity of the **subjugation** of blacks.

THE MISSOURI COMPROMISE

The United States' first major conflict of the 1800s that required a legislative solution began when Missouri sought admission into the Union. Since no restrictions on the spread of slavery into the territory of the Louisiana Purchase had been put into place, debate raged between supporters and opponents of slavery over whether to allow the territory of Missouri to enter the Union as a slave state.

Prior to the request by Missouri's settlers for admission to the Union in 1819, the balance between slave and free states stood evenly divided, with eleven of each. Northerners held that Congress could prohibit slavery in a new state, but Southerners believed that all new states had the same freedom to choose to allow slavery as the original thirteen states. The argument grew

Scan here to learn more about the Missouri Compromise.

rife with sectional discord, until Senator Henry Clay proposed a compromise bill.

Under the provisions of the Missouri Compromise, the equal balance between slave and free states would be maintained by admitting Missouri as a slave state, and Maine, which had formerly been part of Massachusetts, would enter as a free state. Additionally, all lands north of latitude 36°30´ in the western territories would remain free of slavery.

Ostensibly, the Missouri Compromise maintained not only the balance between free and slave states in the Union, but also cooled sectional tensions for a time. It would not be long, however, before another crisis loomed—this time over how far the jurisdiction of the federal government could reach without violating the rights of states to make their own laws.

THE NULLIFICATION CRISIS

The United States levied a series of **tariffs** after the end of the War of 1812 to generate revenue for the government and provide some protections to American manufacturers that would otherwise be affected by low-cost imports from Europe. These tariffs disproportionately affected Southern economies that were based

The Missouri Compromise of 1820 limited the western territories in which slavery would be permitted.

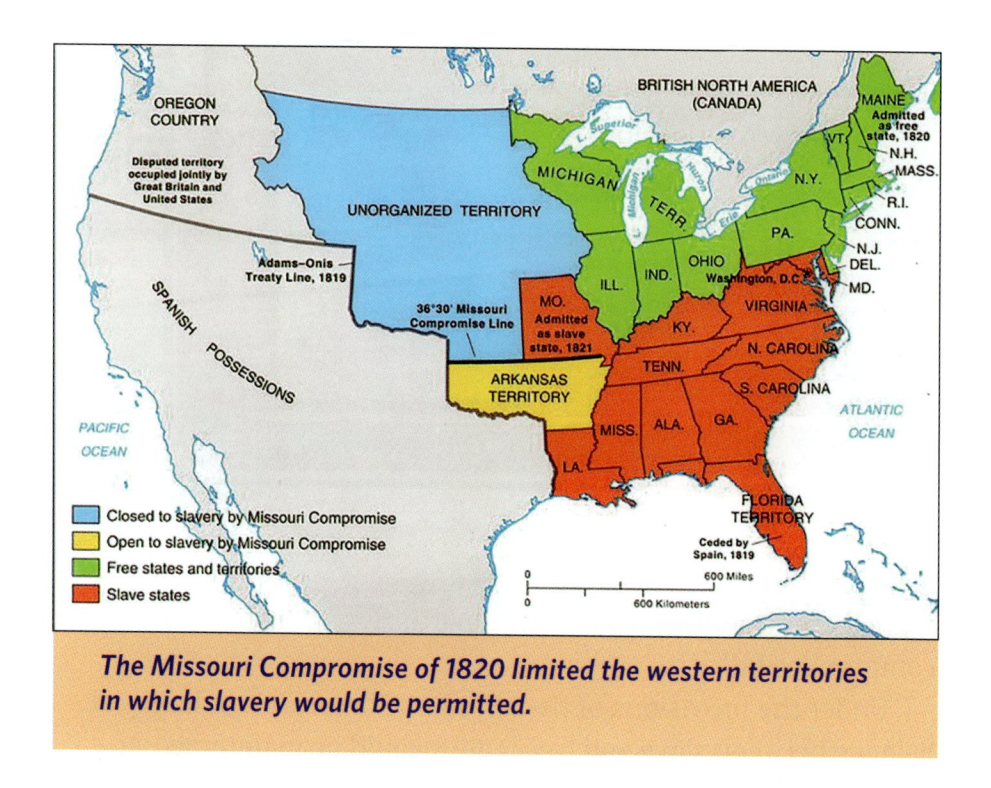

on agriculture rather than industry, as they increased the price of necessary goods brought into Southern states. In addition, the chance that Great Britain, the primary purchaser for Southern cotton, would reduce how much cotton it would import for its textile mills created economic worries for planters.

Northern states with economies based on ever-increasing industrialization generally supported the tariffs. But in the South, many came to feel the tariffs posed an unfair burden and exceeded the authority of the federal government. The concept of nullification, in which the states had the right to ignore federal laws if such legislation overstepped the confines of the Constitution, began to gain traction.

In 1828, then vice president John C. Calhoun anonymously wrote a letter of protest on behalf of his native South Carolina, maintaining that the states were not required to enforce the tariff passed in that same year. Calhoun also believed that states

John C. Calhoun, a politician from South Carolina, was a powerful supporter of slavery. He developed the theory that because the states had agreed to form the United States, a state had the power to nullify, or reject, federal laws that it disagreed with.

had veto power over federal law to protect the minority from the actions of the majority, blocking enforcement of any law that was not made into a constitutional amendment. Four years later, South Carolina lawmakers adopted the Ordinance of Nullification, declaring that "the several acts and parts of the acts of the Congress of the United States . . . imposing duties on imports . . . are unauthorized by the constitution . . . are utterly null and void." In addition, the ordinance threatened secession should force be used to enforce the tariffs.

The federal government's response foreshadowed the conflict of years to come. President Jackson issued a proclamation addressing South Carolina's claims, asserting the federal governments supremacy in matters of law, and warning that an attempt to secede through the use of armed force would be considered treason. Congress followed Jackson's proclamation with the Force Bill of 1833, which authorized the use of military force if necessary, and a compromise tariff that reduced the duties currently in place. South Carolina rescinded the Ordinance of Secession but nullified the Force Bill.

The nullification crisis aggravated the growing conflict between Southern and Northern states, while also planting the seeds of disunion. South Carolina had attempted to bring other Southern states join them in nullifying federal laws. Though the attempt failed, many Southerners began to mull the idea that secession, despite Jackson's warning, may be the only sure way to protect the interests of their states.

THE ANNEXATION OF TEXAS AND ACQUISITION OF MEXICAN TERRITORY

While the United States grappled with tariffs and the nullification crisis, its neighbor to the southwest was in the throes of revolution and rebellion. Mexico won its independence from Spain in 1821, but by the early 1830s, it was already experiencing its own crisis of disunion.

American settlers began moving, with the approval of the Mexican government, into the region north of the Rio Grande,

THE GUERRERO DECREE

The Spanish brought African slaves to Mexico after conquering the lands once ruled by the Aztecs, and the rigid **encomienda system** made slavery an integral part of Mexico's social structure. After winning independence, president Vicente Guerrero issued a decree abolishing slavery in the Republic of Mexico, except for the Isthmus of Tehuantepec, which is in the southeast of the modern-day Mexican state of Oaxaca.

The 1829 decree immediately caused consternation among proslavery settlers in Texas, who petitioned for an exemption from the law. The petition was denied, although the decree itself was not ultimately enforced. Mexico did not abolish slavery until 1831.

in what is now the state of Texas, in the 1820s and 1830s. These settlers had to agree to be loyal to the Mexican government, learn Spanish, and convert to Roman Catholicism. The distance between Texas and the central government in Mexico City allowed most of the settlers the freedom to ignore these conditions. Land grants from the Mexican government drew increasing numbers of Americans, who saw in the fertile soil of Texas the opportunity to grow wealthy through cotton production. Many of these settlers were slaveowners and soon outnumbered the native Tejanos. Mexico's government realized its mistake in allowing the migration of American settlers, but it was too late.

Tensions between the Mexican government and Americans in Texas continued to increase after the abolition of slavery in Mexico in 1831. Then, immigration to Texas was outlawed, and heavy tariffs on imports of foreign goods were enacted. Finally, General Santa Anna's rise to power in 1833 created a consolidation of power and national unity that alarmed Americans in Texas who had grown used to autonomy.

Led by unhappy American settlers, Texas fought against Santa Anna's army and ultimately won its independence from Mexico in 1836. Many in the US public openly supported the move, and Texas's first (and only) president, Samuel Houston, repealed the prohibition on slavery. Annexation by the United States came next, with support both from Texans, who realized the economic and diplomatic challenges of independence, and proslavery Americans who saw opportunity in acquiring another slave state.

The United States ultimately annexed Texas as a slave state, despite the outcry from Northerners who opposed slavery and concern from those who feared war with Mexico should Texas be admitted to the Union. War with Mexico did, indeed, break out in 1846, with many in the proslavery camp seeing an opportunity in potential land acquisition to again expand the institution of slavery and strengthen their economic opportunities.

Even while the war was underway, however, congressman

Pennsylvania congressman David Wilmot was a Democrat in the 1840s, when he proposed a measure to prohibit slavery in new western territories acquired from Mexico. He would later help to create the Republican Party in the mid-1850s.

David Wilmot of Pennsylvania introduced a proviso attached to an appropriations bill that provided funds for negotiations with Mexico, which state that, in any lands acquired from Mexico that "neither slavery nor involuntary servitude shall ever exist in any part of said territory." The bill passed twice in the House of Representatives, but the Senate first did not take action on the proviso, and then it was defeated in the Senate due to John C. Calhoun's opposition to it.

The Wilmot Proviso created yet another split in the growing rift between North and South, free and slave. More and more Northerners opposed the expansion of slavery into new territories, while many Southerners believed the institution should be legal everywhere. The specter of economic competition between slaveowners and small farmers grew, and a growing moral argument against slavery empowered the abolitionist movement. In addition, the proviso's conditions eventually became a backbone of the Free Soil Party and, later, the Republican Party.

TEXT-DEPENDENT QUESTIONS

1. What motivated the acquisition of the Louisiana Purchase?
2. Why did Missouri's request to join the Union as a slave state create conflict?
3. What drew American settlers into Texas?
4. How did the annexation of Texas and acquisition of land after the Mexican War fuel sectional tensions?

RESEARCH PROJECT

Using your school library and internet resources, gather primary and secondary source documents about the Missouri Compromise, annexation of Texas, and the land in the Southwest gained after the Mexican War. Then choose one side of the argument, and, acting as a member of a congressional committee in 1848, prepare a two- to three-page report presenting the pros and cons of allowing slavery to expand into the newly acquired, former Mexican territory of the Southwest.

Slaves pick cotton on a plantation in Mississippi. By the 1840s, cotton was the most profitable cash crop produced in the United States.

WORDS TO UNDERSTAND

The **cotton gin** was a machine that separated cotton seeds from cotton fibers in preparation for spinning into thread for textiles.

Federalism (in the United States) is a principle of government in which the power of governance is distributed between a central government and the governments of the states.

The concept of **Manifest Destiny** was a nineteenth-century belief that the United States' expansion across the North American continent was justified and inevitable.

Secession is the act of formally withdrawing from membership of a federation or political state.

CHAPTER 3

A Deepening Divide

By the end of the 1840s, territorial gains exacerbated the growing tensions between different sections of the country. Proslavery Southerners wanted to see the institution of slavery follow the path of manifest destiny, a phrase coined in 1845 but a concept born long before. **Manifest destiny** centered on the belief that Americans were meant to "overspread the continent allotted by Providence for the free development of our yearly multiplying millions." For supporters of slavery, manifest destiny was no only about land, but about economic opportunities and the right they believed they had to bring slavery into those new lands for the purpose of economic prosperity.

    The growth of "King Cotton" as cash crop enriched more than just the slave owners of the United States in the early to mid-1800s. The Industrial Revolution thrived on cotton textiles, and demand for cotton soared in the industrial centers of the American Northeast as well as Great Britain and other parts of Europe. By 1840, the American South produced 60 percent of the cotton used worldwide; almost 70 percent of the British textile industry's supply of cotton came from the United States. Eli Whitney's invention of the **cotton gin** in 1793 made the process of preparing cotton for manufacture easier, but in the process allowed for greater cotton production overall. As a result, the demand for slave labor to grow that cotton increased as well.

Scan here to learn more about the cotton economy and slavery.

    Slavery affected more than just rural agricultural areas. Slaves served in households as maids, cooks, butlers, and nursemaids, and many developed the skilled labor of tradesmen like blacksmiths, carpenters, and tailors. Still others were sailors and fishermen. Most urban slaves worked for their owners but some were hired out to other slave owners, factories, or municipal authorities. A small percentage of slaves could hire themselves out and paid some of their earnings to their owners; the ability to hire oneself out created the opportunity to earn money that, potentially, allowed the slave to buy his own freedom or that of his family.

    Slaves were seen by their owners, and by proponents of the institution, as property, and the law treated them as such. As such, they could be bought and sold for profit, used as collateral in business transactions, traded in exchange for goods and services, or to pay off debts. The sale of slaves also produced tax revenue at the state and local level, and the value of estates included the value of the slaves.

    The economic impact of slavery was profound, and as the 1800s wore on toward their midpoint, the institution became ever more entrenched. Politics, too, were increasingly tied to slavery as sectional differences deepened and political parties began to fracture. On both sides of the issue, people worked to either enshrine slavery or to dismantle it.

GROWTH OF ABOLITION

Abolitionist organizations existed before the American Revolution, but it was not until the third decade of the 1800s that the movement to abolish American slavery truly took off. The main goal of abolitionists was to immediately free all slaves and end race-based segregation and discrimination. Opposition to the westward expansion of slavery was an important goal as well, though this was more the focus of the Free Soil movement that did not necessarily seek to end slavery where it already existed.

The American Anti-Slavery Society was born in 1833, when a group of men and women, both black and white, met in Philadelphia with the express purpose of founding a society aimed at ending slavery in America forever. They denounced slavery as a moral sin and condemned racial prejudice, while promoting non-violent means to achieve their ends. Within two years, the society had grown to include hundreds more branches in free states across the North, with support from free African American communities

This illustration of a chained male slave pleading for freedom was used on abolitionist publications in the 1830s and 1840s.

DID YOU KNOW?

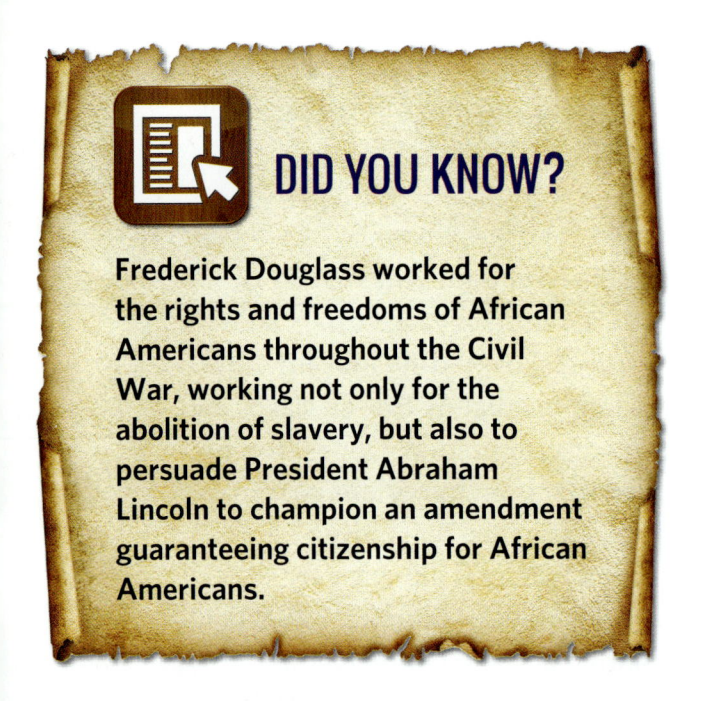

Frederick Douglass worked for the rights and freedoms of African Americans throughout the Civil War, working not only for the abolition of slavery, but also to persuade President Abraham Lincoln to champion an amendment guaranteeing citizenship for African Americans.

as well. The society used a variety of publications to spread its message and petitioned Congress to end federal support for slavery. These petitions eventually led to the passage of a "gag rule" in the House of Repesentatives, which banned even the discussion of antislavery petitions from the House floor.

Escaped slaves who were able to make a new home in the free states of the North joined the abolitionist movement, using their own stories to illustrate the horrors suffered by those in bondage in the South. Frederick Douglass, for example, gave numerous speeches about his experiences and published an antislavery newspaper, *The North Star*, to spread the message of the abolitionist movement through essays, letters, and notices of meetings. The masthead of *The North Star* clearly stated its purpose, in alignment with the greater abolitionist movement, was "to attack slavery in all its forms and aspects; advocate universal emancipation; exalt the standard of public morality; promote the moral and intellectual improvement of the colored people; and hasten the day of freedom to the three millions of our enslaved fellow countrymen."

The abolitionist movement faced hostility from many sides, including in the North where racial tensions developed between free African Americans and immigrants from countries like Ireland and Germany. The movement faced its own internal strife, too, as members disagreed on such things as women's rights. Despite this, the movement gained political and social traction, drawing on views of morality and using popular literature to educate the masses about slavery's atrocities, and founding racially integrated schools such as Oberlin College. Politically, abolitionists promoted antislavery candidates for public office, and the eventual creation of the Republican Party came from a combination of several other political parties that held the opposition to slavery as a core part of their platforms.

STATES' RIGHTS AND SECESSIONISM

The core of the Nullification Crisis of the 1830s rested on the belief that the several states had the ability and right to veto or override any federal law that they perceived to be an overextension of the federal governments constitutional authority. This, over the 1840s and 1850s, would morph into the States' Rights platform that shaped further sectionalism and fed into a growing movement for **secession**.

The States' Rights doctrine was based on an interpretation of the Tenth Amendment to the Constitution. The amendment helps to enshrine the concept of **federalism**, and states that "powers not delegated to the United States by the Constitution, nor prohibited by it to the states, are reserved to the states respectively, or to the people." The interpretation promoted by States' Rights advocates (and later secessionists) held that the federal government could not interfere in the affairs of individual states, and was a direct product of the nullification crisis.

Though primarily about protecting the regional interests of the South, interests that were built upon the perpetuation of slavery for social and economic reasons, the States' Rights movement also led to the push for secession. John C. Calhoun, during the nullification crisis, not only linked States' Rights to slavery but also proposed that the states could cut ties with the federal government if its policies were detrimental to the states' self-interests. As the 1850s continued and tensions continued to grow,

DEFINING CITIZENSHIP

In 1857, the Supreme Court ruled on a case that determined, for a time, whether or not blacks could be considered citizens of the United States.

A slave named Dred Scott had been taken by his owner from Missouri, a slave state, into Illinois, a free state and then into the Wisconsin Territory, a free territory. Though Scott eventually returned to Missouri with his owner, he sued for his freedom, stating that because he had resided in free lands north of the Missouri Compromise line, he should be granted his freedom.

A series of lower court decisions first declared Scott to be free, then the decision reversed. The case made its way to the US Supreme Court, where Chief Justice Roger Taney argued that state citizenship did not equate with national citizenship, and that African Americans could not sue in federal court because they could not be US citizens. Further, after a string of difficult reasoning, Taney determined that Scott's status depended on local law, and since he had returned to Missouri, he would again be considered a slave—and thus without citizenship.

The decision was rejected in Northern courts but lauded in Southern courts. The question of citizenship for African Americans would not be settled until the passage of the Fourteenth Amendment, which states that "all persons born or naturalized in the United States, and subject to the jurisdiction thereof, are citizens of the United States."

many parts of the South began to promote the view that it might be in their best interests to secede.

FUGITIVE SLAVE LAWS

Between 1793 and 1850, the US Congress passed two fugitive slaves laws, which authorized local governments to capture escaped slaves and return them to their owners. These laws also carried penalties for anyone who helped these slaves in their attempt to gain freedom in another state or territory.

The first Fugitive Slave Act of 1793 came about after multiple northern states abolished slavery during and immediately following the American Revolution. Southern politicians sought a way to keep these free states from becoming havens for runaway slaves, and looked to the Constitution for answers. They found one in a "fugitive slave clause" in Article 4, Section 2, Clause 3, which held that no one held in "service or labor" would be set free if they managed to escape to a free state. Congress passed the first Fugitive Slave Act under pressure from Southern politicians and in spite of protest against it by Northern lawmakers.

This first law provided more details on how the fugitive slave clause in the Constitution should be enforced, but also decreed that slave owners could search, either on their own or through the help of hired agents, for escaped slaves within the borders of free states. Slave owners did have to prove in court that they owned the suspected runaway, but a signed affidavit often sufficed. Many free blacks were kidnapped into slavery during this time.

Furious Northern states ignored the fugitive slave law, despite court decisions ruling that federal law superseded state laws that interfered with the enforcement of the Fugitive Slave Act. Secret networks, most famously the Underground Railroad, developed across the country, and thousands of slaves used these networks to reach free states and Canada by the mid-1800s.

In response to pressure from the South, a stricter Fugitive Slave Act was passed as part of the Compromise of 1850. Under the new law, citizens were forced to help capture runaway slaves, denied slaves the right to a trial by jury, and increased penalties for those who tried to interfere. Some states attempted to bypass or nullify the new law, antislavery riots erupted, and abolitionists increased their efforts to help fugitives. The law became unenforceable but remained in effect until June of 1864.

BIRTH OF THE REPUBLICAN PARTY

American politics shifted during the three decades leading up to the outbreak of the Civil War, as proslavery factions in the South pushed economic and political agendas in Congress. New political parties developed while others fractured; the Democratic-Republican Party of Thomas Jefferson evolved in the 1830s to be come the Democratic Party. In the two decades before the Civil War, the Democratic Party's platform consisted of, among other goals, the maintenance of slavery in the South and, for some factions, its expansion into western territories.

Former Democrats who did not support slavery soon joined with members of the former Whig Party and the Free Soil Party. They formed the new Republican Party in the 1850s. Their platform called for the abolition of slavery in the territories, which garnered a large amount of support in the North. The Republicans soon replaced what was left of the Whig party as the Democratic Party's main political foe. Through the 1850s, the Republican Party solidified its stance on abolishing slavery, and a new candidate emerged: Abraham Lincoln.

TEXT-DEPENDENT QUESTIONS

1. How did the Industrial Revolution impact slavery in America?
2. What methods did the Anti-Slavery Society use to spread their message and gain support?
3. What was the principle behind States' Rights?
4. How did the Fugitive Slave Acts of 1793 and 1850 cause division between the North and the South?

RESEARCH PROJECT

Gather and examine primary and secondary sources about the Anti-Slavery Society's activity from the 1830s-1850s and the Civil Rights Movement of the 1950s and 1960s. Write a four-page research paper comparing and contrasting the abolitionist movement with the Civil Rights Movement, focusing on: 1.) the principles and goals each movement hoped to achieve; 2.) methods used by each movement's leaders; 3.) the comparative effectiveness of their methods for the time; and 4.) the legacy and/or roadmap each movement left for future activist movements to follow.

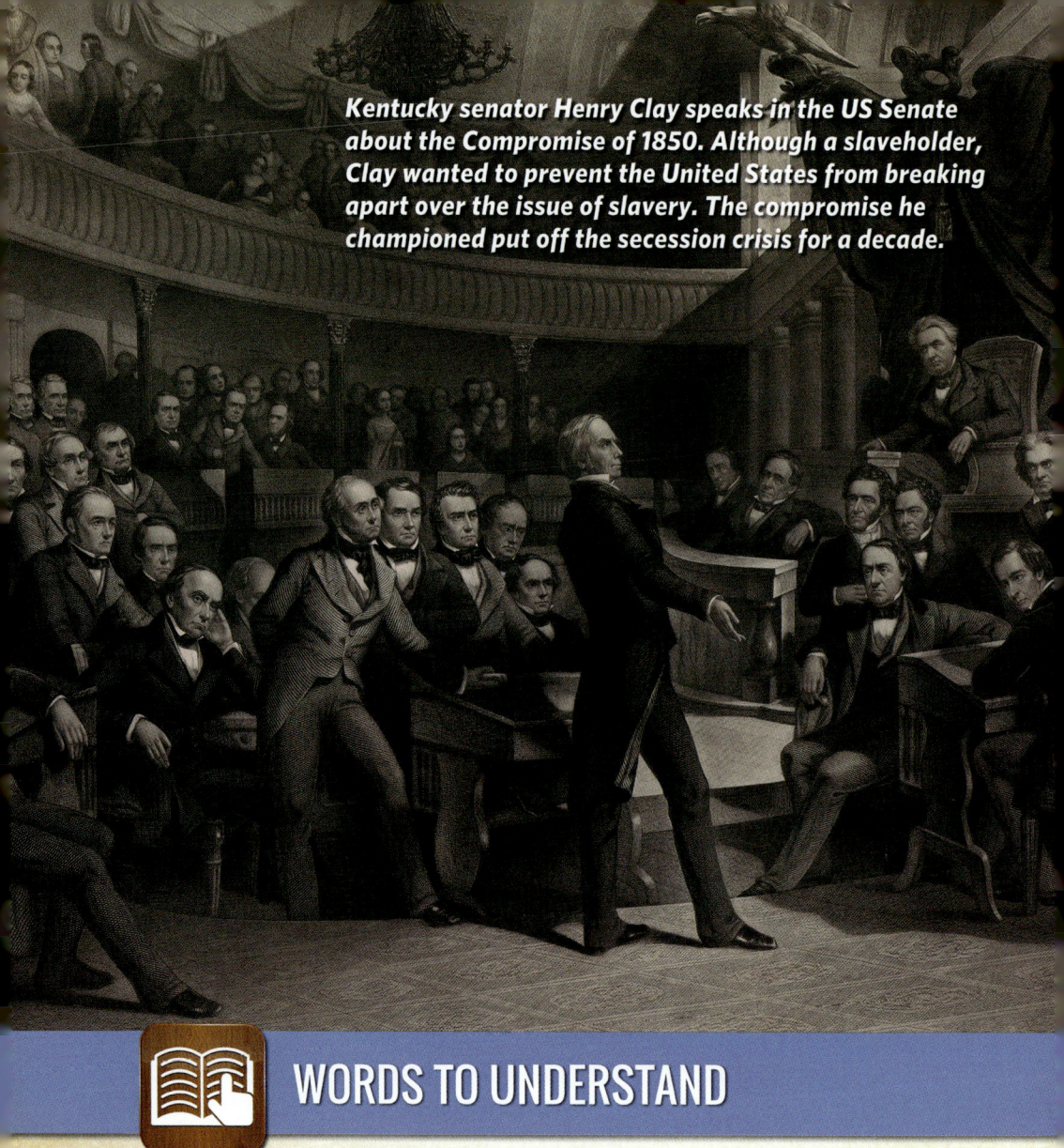

Kentucky senator Henry Clay speaks in the US Senate about the Compromise of 1850. Although a slaveholder, Clay wanted to prevent the United States from breaking apart over the issue of slavery. The compromise he championed put off the secession crisis for a decade.

WORDS TO UNDERSTAND

An **insurrection** is a violent uprising or revolt against a government or authority.

Lynching refers to the killing of someone for an alleged crime with or without due process; typically refers to such killings by hanging but includes any method of extrajudicial killing.

Popular sovereignty is a political doctrine asserting that the government is created by and subject to the will of the people.

CHAPTER 4

From Bleeding Kansas to Harper's Ferry

The decade immediately preceding the Civil War tested the bonds of Union literally to the breaking point. The abolitionist movement gained considerable support in the North, even from sectors of the population that may not have agreed with racial equality under the law but derided the institution of slavery as a moral wrong. At the same time, the doctrine of States' Rights became increasingly popular among Southerners who viewed the perpetuation of slavery as both a social and economic necessity.

Tensions ran high after the Mexican War, and the territorial gains of the peace treaty proved too valuable on both sides of the free/slave argument to maintain the balance of the Missouri Compromise. A new compromise was needed if the Union was to stay together.

THE COMPROMISE OF 1850

The California Gold Rush of 1849 resulted in a surge of population and petitioned Congress to enter the Union as a free state. With the balance of free and slave states now in jeopardy, a new crisis loomed. Senator Henry Clay, one of the chief architects of the Missouri Compromise of 1820, presented a series of potential compromises before Congress in an attempt to pacify angry Southerners and prevent the further degradation of sectional

Slave catchers corner runaways in a Maryland barn. The Fugitive Slave Act, passed as part of the Compromise of 1850, required northerners to help return escaped slaves to their owners. The law was very controversial in the North.

relations. With him in debating a palatable compromise were John C. Calhoun and Daniel Webster, and the resulting legislation moved through Congress with the support of a rising Democratic senator from Illinois, Stephen Douglas.

The Compromise of 1850 contained five separate bills designed to diffuse tensions and, ostensibly, make both sides of the argument happy. California's petition to enter the union as a free state was approved, while no restrictions on slavery would be enforced in the territories of Utah or New Mexico. California's admission as a free state was also offset by a new Fugitive Slave Act that strengthened its 1793 predecessor. This move appeased Southerners but upset Northerners and bolstered the abolitionist movement into greater, urgent action. In addition, land disputes involving Texas's claim to territory extending all the way to Santa Fe in New Mexico was resolved by compensating Texas with $10 million dollars. Finally, slavery remained legal in Washington, D.C., but the capital's participation in the domestic slave trade was prohibited.

Neither Henry Clay nor John C. Calhoun lived long enough to see the bitter fruits of their long-debated attempt at compromise. For a time, the United States settled into an uneasy peace. But tensions still simmered, and, within four years, another dispute over slavery in the territories launched the country another step closer to civil war.

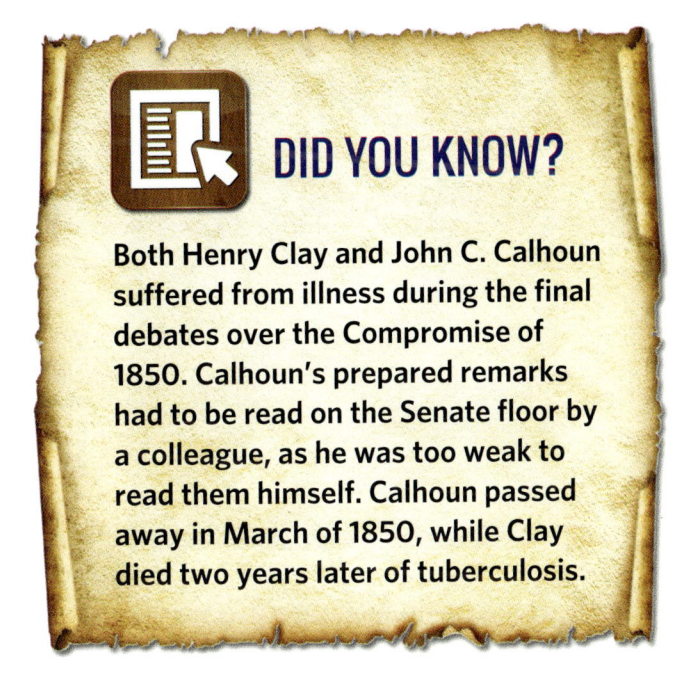

> **DID YOU KNOW?**
>
> Both Henry Clay and John C. Calhoun suffered from illness during the final debates over the Compromise of 1850. Calhoun's prepared remarks had to be read on the Senate floor by a colleague, as he was too weak to read them himself. Calhoun passed away in March of 1850, while Clay died two years later of tuberculosis.

THE KANSAS-NEBRASKA ACT

The Compromise of 1850 opened the possibility of slavery's eventual expansion in the Utah and New Mexico territories, but the use of latitude as part of the Missouri Compromise remained in effect in determining whether western territories could be free or slave. When the race to build a transcontinental railroad got underway, political aims stoked the fires of sectionalism once again.

Stephen Douglas hoped the transcontinental railroad would benefit his home state of Illinois if a northern route linked the states of the East with the Pacific coast, and as such moved to promote a bill organizing the territory of Nebraska. Senators from the South argued that the bill would make the territory free soil, as it lay north of latitude 36°30′. To gain Southern support, Douglas offered what would become the Kansas-Nebraska Act: the area

In the 1850s, Illinois Senator Stephen A. Douglas wanted to let the people who settled in the western territories decide whether slavery should be permitted. This principle, which Douglas included in the Kansas-Nebraska Act of 1854, made it possible for slave states to be created above the 36°30′ line established by the Missouri Compromise.

would be divided into two territories of Kansas and Nebraska, the Missouri Compromise line would be repealed, and the status of slavery in the territories would be left up to the settlers under the principle of **popular sovereignty**.

Supported by president Franklin Pierce and southern lawmakers, the legislation passed. The fallout was immediate, both in terms of politics as well as stability within the territory in question. Members of the Free Soil party in Congress used newspapers to attack the president and Senator Douglas for the repeal of the Missouri Compromise. Independent Democrats and northern Whigs left their parties to join the Republican Party, which adhered to the core principle of ending slavery. Whigs in the South lost political allies, and the Democratic Party split further into factions.

Within the Kansas and Nebraska territories, however, a conflict arose that forged more bitterness between rival sections of the country and foreshadowed the terrible war that would follow in less than a decade.

"BLEEDING KANSAS"

As soon as the two new territories opened to settlement, antislavery and proslavery settlers rushed to the region, each side keen to establish a majority that would give them the voting power to decide whether Kansas and Nebraska would be free or slave. Additionally, some who moved to Kansas not only wished to see the territory free from slavery, but also free of African Americans in general.

What had been a mostly verbal and legislative dispute up until now quickly erupted into violence and bloodshed. Settlers on both sides of the political argument found themselves the victims of guerilla warfare and retaliation. For example, an 1856 attack on the town of Lawrence, carried out by proslavery settlers, prompted an attack by anti-slavery settlers living on Pottawatomie Creek. The leader of this retaliatory attack was John Brown; his actions in May 1856 led to the nicknaming of the region as "Bleeding Kansas."

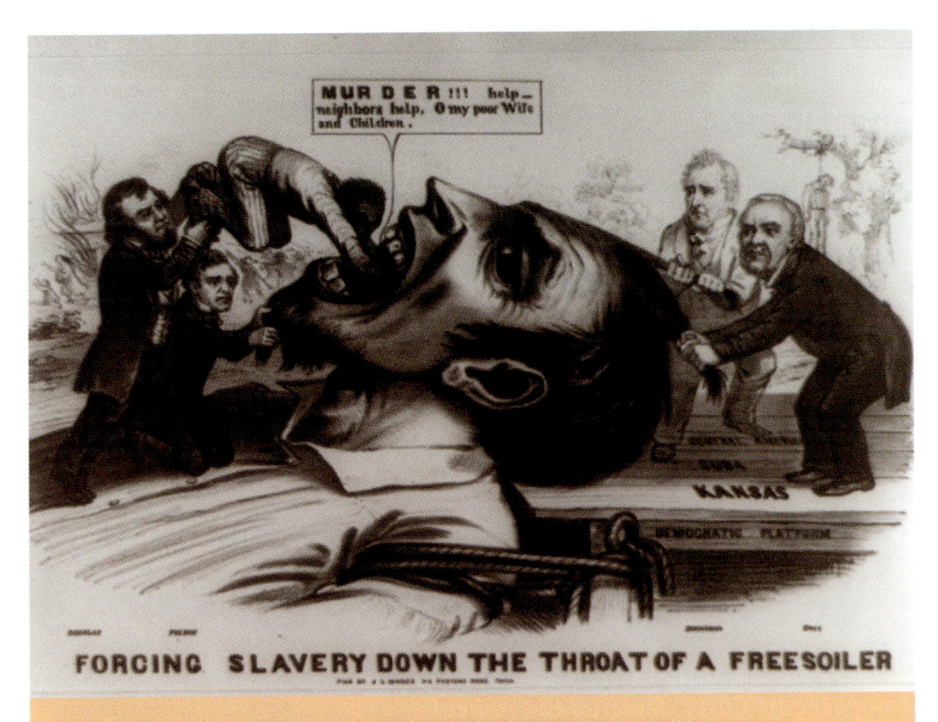

A political cartoon from the mid-1850s depicts Stephen A. Douglas and other Democrats forcing a black man into the mouth of an anti-slavery ("Free Soil") settler in Kansas.

JOHN BROWN'S WAR

In the five years leading up to the secession of the Southern states, one of the most notorious men in the sectional conflict was John Brown. Born in Connecticut and raised in Ohio, Brown became heavily involved in the abolitionist movement, serving as a conductor on the Underground Railroad and organizing a group tasked with helping free blacks and runaway slaves protect themselves. When Kansas opened for settlement, Brown moved there with five of his sons, determined to see the territory enter the Union as a free state.

Brown was not only an abolitionist, he was a radical one. While many branches of the Anti-Slavery Society espoused nonviolence as a means to an end, Brown believed that slavery was a scourge upon America and must be cleansed through bloodshed. Further, he came to believe that he had been chosen by God to lead slaves into freedom, by any means necessary.

The clash at Pottawatomie Creek was only the beginning for Brown; he also led armed raids into Missouri. His methods alienated many abolitionists who might have supported him in theory, but others joined his cause. In 1858, he began planning his final act to end slavery in America, one that proved his most infamous—the raid on Harper's Ferry.

In this painting of John Brown, artist John Steuart Curry depicted the radical abolitionist with a crazed expression and an enslaved African American at his side. A powerful storm is coming.

CAUSES OF THE CIVIL WAR

CLASH AT HARPER'S FERRY

Between 1858 and 1859, John Brown began a grand plan to lead a massive slave **insurrection** in Virginia. His plan revolved around the seizure of a federal arsenal in Harper's Ferry, a town on the banks of the Potomac River, which he believed would prompt hundreds of slaves to rebel against their owners and join him in creating an army. His newly armed force of rebelling slaves would then march south, sparking further slave uprisings along the way. Brown even went so far as to write a provisional constitution for his hoped-for revolutionary state, "the better to protect our persons, property, lives, and liberties, and to govern our actions".

The raid itself proved to be a failure. Brown and 18 of his followers attacked the arsenal and took prisoners, but word of the rebellion did not spread as Brown intended. Instead, a contingent of US Marines under the command of Colonel Robert E. Lee—who would later lead the Confederate Army of Northern Virginia—responded with force and captured Brown and the surviving members of his band after an exchange of gunfire.

The governor of Virginia wished to see Brown receive a speedy

To learn more about John Brown's raid on Harper's Ferry, scan here.

trial in order to circumvent the possibilities of either a **lynching** or a rescue. The trial commenced after a week, and Brown's defense lawyer attempted to argue that Brown suffered from insanity. Brown protested this, hoping to turn his trial into a platform from which he could attack the institution of slavery. The trial ended with a charge of treason, and Brown was sentenced to hang. In his final statement, Brown asserted that his only aim had been to free the slaves, even if it required fighting to do so; as he ascended the gallows for his execution, he declared that "the crimes of this guilty land will never be purged away, but with blood."

Brown's raid on Harper's Ferry and the exposure of his planned slave insurrection infuriated Southerners. At the same time, Brown became a martyr to the abolitionist cause, and the raid ushered in one last year of ever increasing discord that became a turning point for American history.

Abolitionist John Brown ascends the scaffold to be hung for leading the Harper's Ferry insurrection.

TEXT-DEPENDENT QUESTIONS

1. How did the Compromise of 1850 attempt to ease political and sectional tensions?
2. How did the Kansas-Nebraska Act exacerbate sectional discord?
3. Why did John Brown lead attacks on proslavery settlers in Kansas?
4. What were the results of the raid on Harper's Ferry?

RESEARCH PROJECT

Examine newspaper articles, available court transcripts, letters, and other primary source documents about the Harper's Ferry raid and John Brown's trial. Using these sources contemporary to the time, prepare either:

1. A new case for the prosecution, focusing on how John Brown's actions affected political attempts to prevent disunion and find a compromised legislative solution to slavery in America; or
2. A new case of for the defense, focusing on how John Brown's actions were necessary to spur the country's lawmakers to act on the institution of slavery.

THE NATIONAL GAME. THREE "OUTS" AND ONE "RUN"
ABRAHAM WINNING THE BALL.

WORDS TO UNDERSTAND

The **Electoral College** of the United States is a body of representatives that formally casts votes for the election of the president and vice president; the awarding of electoral votes is based on the outcome of the popular vote in each state.

An **ordinance** is an authoritative decree or law established by a governing body.

A **provisional government** is an emergency government authority that manages political transitions, such as in the establishment of new nations or when a previous government collapses.

CHAPTER 5

The Election of 1860 and Secession Winter

While the legislation of the 1850s unsuccessfully attempted to prevent sectional discord, violence in Kansas and John Brown's raid on the federal arsenal served to deepen the divide between free and slave to a mortal level. But as the decade drew to a close and the election of 1860 loomed on the horizon, the political landscape began to shift, and the Republican Party, with its staunch antislavery platform, took center stage.

THE LINCOLN-DOUGLAS DEBATES

Abraham Lincoln was the epitome of a self-made man, having taught himself not only to read but also the intricacies of the law. A relatively unknown lawyer from Illinois, he had gained popularity among Republicans by the middle of the 1850s. Lincoln faced off with Democrat Stephen Douglas in 1858 in that year's bid for one of Illinois's seats in the US Senate.

Lincoln stated in his speech accepting the Republican nomination that the government of the United States could not

Opposite: This political cartoon published a few weeks before the 1860 presidential election depicts Abraham Lincoln as the winner in a four-way game of baseball. Lincoln's "good bat" is actually a wooden fence rail labeled "Equal Rights and Free Territory."

LINCOLN'S CHANGING VIEWS ON SLAVERY

Throughout his adult life and public career, Abraham Lincoln's views on slavery changed dramatically. He considered himself to be against slavery's expansion into western territories from the beginning of his political career, but did not advocate for immediate and total emancipation of slaves where the institution already existed.

Lincoln believed that slavery existed due to social justifications on the part of its proponents. In a fragment of writing in 1854, he addressed arguments that slavery was proper based on the color or intellect of slaves:

> Take care. By this rule, you are to be slave to the first man you meet, with a fairer skin than your own.
>
> You do not mean color exactly? You mean the whites are intellectually the superiors of the blacks, and, therefore have the right to enslave them? Take care again. By this rule, you are to be slave to the first man you meet, with an intellect superior to your own.
>
> But, say you, it is a question of interest; and, if you can make it your interest; you have the right to enslave another. Very well. And if he can make it his interest, he has the right to enslave you.

Lincoln unequivocally believed slavery was wrong, but struggled with what should be done about it. The idea of sending African Americans back to Africa had his support for a time, as he viewed blacks as a people who had been uprooted from their homeland and unjustly brought to America in the first place. He also supported gradual emancipation coupled with compensation for slave owners.

When the Civil War started, Lincoln resisted calls to push for emancipation of slaves. By the end of the war, however, Lincoln firmly believed in the necessity of abolishing slavery, paving the way for the passage of the Thirteenth Amendment.

"endure permanently half slave and half free." Douglas asserted that Lincoln's thinking was radical and harmful to the stability of the nation; in response, Lincoln challenged Douglas to a series of seven debates throughout Illinois.

The debates revolved around the extension of slavery into the territories, with Douglas consistently trying to label Lincoln as an advocate for racial equality and disunion. Lincoln, in turn, focused on the immorality of slavery and pointed out the effect popular sovereignty had had on Kansas in the preceding years. When challenged to explain how popular sovereignty could exist alongside the Dred Scott decision—under which states and territories could not prohibit slavery—Douglas maintained that proslavery settlers simply wouldn't bring slaves into a territory, if free soil settlers simply failed to provide enforcement for such local regulations as a slave code that protected protect a slaveowner's property. Douglas's so-called "Freeport Doctrine" would prove disastrous for his future campaign to win the White House in 1860.

THE ELECTION OF 1860

Stephen Douglas's stance put forth by the Freeport Doctrine angered Southern Democrats and brought them to the conclusion

Scan here to learn more about the election of 1860.

that, despite his support of slavery, Douglas was not the ideal candidate to defeat the Republicans in the upcoming presidential election. This caused a split in the Democratic Party, with Southern Democrats walking out of the convention in April 1860 before a candidate could be nominated. Northern Democrats nominated Stephen Douglas, but Southern Democrats chose vice president John C. Breckinridge to represent their faction.

Both factions believed their candidate capable of winning the presidency. Northern Democrats' platform upheld popular sovereignty but excluded mention of a federal slave code in the territories. On the other hand, Southern Democrats ran a

In addition to Lincoln and Douglas, two other candidates sought the presidency in 1860. John C. Breckinridge (left), the sitting vice president, was nominated by the Southern wing of the Democratic Party. Breckinridge was also appointed to represent Kentucky in the US Senate, but after the 1860 election he supported the Confederacy and became an officer in its army. Americans who hoped for another legislative compromise that would prevent the South from seceeding created the Constitutional Union Party, which nominated former Tennessee Senator John Bell as its presidential candidate in 1860.

Legend:
- Lincoln (Republican)
- Bell (Constitutional Union)
- Douglas (Northern Democratic)
- Breckinridge (Southern Democratic)
- Non-Voting Territories

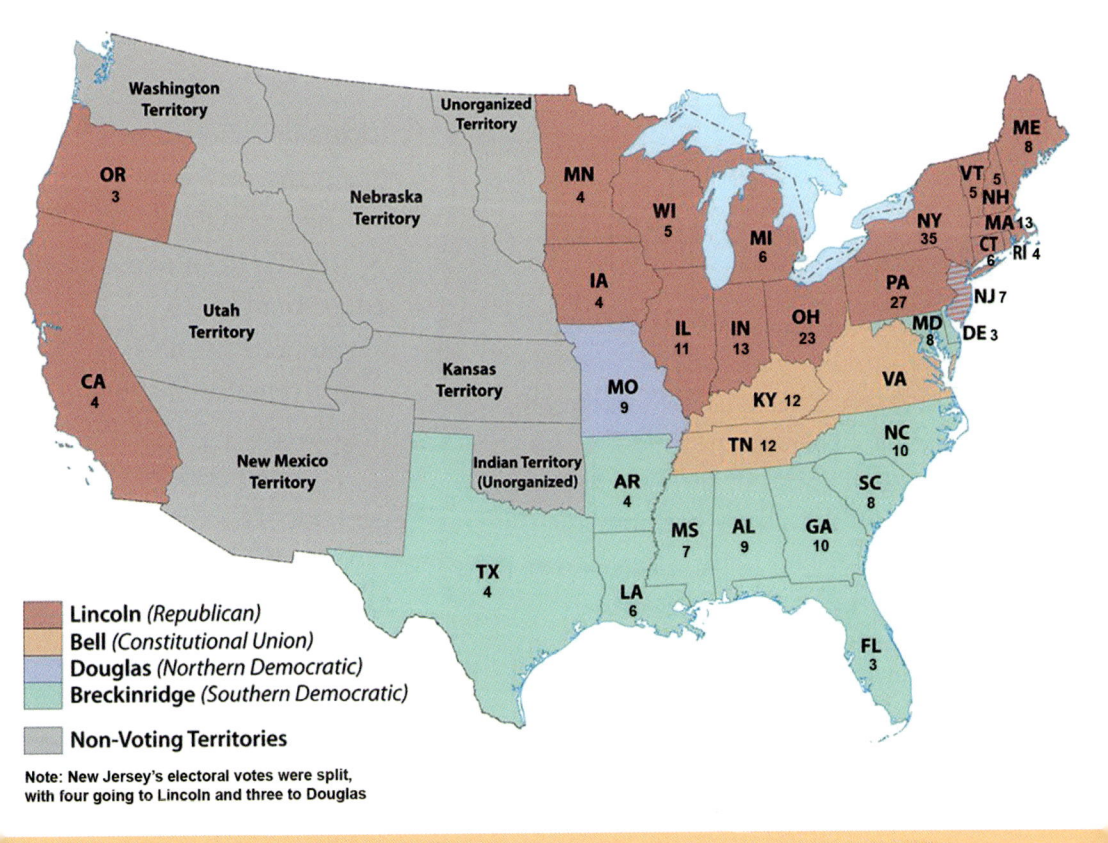

Note: New Jersey's electoral votes were split, with four going to Lincoln and three to Douglas.

> Republican Abraham Lincoln won the 1860 election by carrying seventeen states, for a total of 180 electoral votes. He was followed by John C. Breckinridge (72 electoral votes), John Bell (39 electoral votes), and Stephen A. Douglas (12 electoral votes).

platform built on the right of the federal government to protect slaveholders' interests when settling in a territory.

Voters were further split by the formation of the Constitutional Union Party, which nominated Tennessee slaveholder John Bell as their candidate. The Constitutional Union Party's approach to the sectional conflict dividing the nation was to take no stand on the issues and to act with moderation.

Lincoln won the nomination for the Republican Party's candidate, and the platform adopted by the Republicans asserted that all territory was free under normal conditions, that slavery should not be permitted to expand into new territories, and

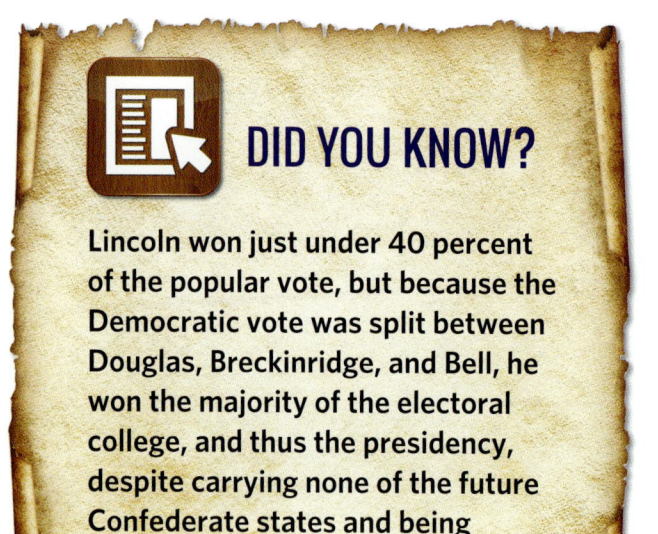

> **DID YOU KNOW?**
>
> Lincoln won just under 40 percent of the popular vote, but because the Democratic vote was split between Douglas, Breckinridge, and Bell, he won the majority of the electoral college, and thus the presidency, despite carrying none of the future Confederate states and being excluded entirely from the ballot in ten southern states.

included endorsement of a transcontinental railroad, growth of industry, and a homestead act that would help encourage the settlement of the territories.

As the election drew closer, even the race for the presidency split between North and South. Lincoln and Douglas essentially competed for votes in northern states, while Bell and Breckinridge looked to win votes in the South. Additionally, Lincoln was vilified in the South; he refused to issue any public statements vowing to uphold slavery where it presently existed, and the Republican Party, with Lincoln as the figurehead, was linked to John Brown's raid on Harper's Ferry. Eventually, sentiment in the South pointed to the justification of secession if Lincoln was elected.

The inability to unify under a single candidate spelled defeat for the Democrats as a whole. Lincoln carried every free state in the Union, while Breckinridge won all the Deep South states and

The front page of the Charleston Mercury from December 20, 1860, reprints an ordinance of secession passed unanimously by a convention of South Carolina leaders. South Carolina was the first state to secede; other Southern states quickly followed.

CHARLESTON MERCURY

EXTRA:

Passed unanimously at 1.15 o'clock, P. M. December 20th, 1860.

AN ORDINANCE

To dissolve the Union between the State of South Carolina and other States united with her under the compact entitled "The Constitution of the United States of America."

We, the People of the State of South Carolina, in Convention assembled, do declare and ordain, and it is hereby declared and ordained,

That the Ordinance adopted by us in Convention, on the twenty-third day of May, in the year of our Lord one thousand seven hundred and eighty-eight, whereby the Constitution of the United States of America was ratified, and also, all Acts and parts of Acts of the General Assembly of this State, ratifying amendments of the said Constitution, are hereby repealed; and that the union now subsisting between South Carolina and other States, under the name of "The United States of America," is hereby dissolved.

THE UNION IS DISSOLVED!

Maryland. Bell won the popular vote in his native Tennessee, as well as Kentucky and Virginia; the only state where Douglas won the majority vote was Missouri.

The results of the election divided the nation before the year was out.

"SECESSION WINTER"

South Carolina, which threatened to secede during the nullification crisis in the 1830s, was the first southern state to issue an **ordinance** of secession on December 20, 1860, cutting ties with the Union after Abraham Lincoln's election. Six other Deep South states soon followed in January and February 1861, joining with South Carolina to form a **provisional government** in Montgomery, Alabama, creating the Confederate States of America.

Some ordinances of secession alluded to the rights of the states to keep slavery legal, but most focused on the termination of the constitutional ties with the United States government. However, the constitution of the Confederacy identified the perpetuation of slavery as a key component of the new nation. Alexander Stephens, who became vice president of the Confederacy, stated in a speech on March 21, 1861, that "the negro is not equal to the white man; that slavery subordination to the superior race is his natural and normal condition."

With the nation thus divided over the issue of slavery, it would only be a matter of time before war would break out.

TEXT-DEPENDENT QUESTIONS

1. What were the main points of the debates between Lincoln and Douglas in 1858?
2. How did Lincoln's views on slavery change over his lifetime?
3. Why did the Democratic Party split into factions in 1860?
4. Why did southern states consider secession to be justified in the event of Lincoln's election?

RESEARCH PROJECT

Using your school library and the internet, gather the texts of the Lincoln-Douglas debates. Acting as a modern-day analyst, evaluate the arguments of each candidate to determine which man "won" the series of debates by having the stronger argument. Then write a two-page report detailing your evaluation, with the inclusion of textual evidence, and create a visual in Google Slides or PowerPoint to organize each candidates' points in the debates.

African-American troops of the 54th Massachusetts Regiment assault Fort Wagner, South Carolina, in 1863.

WORDS TO UNDERSTAND

The **Reconstruction** era, lasting from 1865 to 1877, during which the states that seceded from the United States were reorganized for the purposes of administration and eventual readmission to the Union.

War materiel refers to the equipment and supplies used by a military force.

The **writ of *habeas corpus*** is a requirement that anyone arrested for a crime is to be brought before a court or judge before they can be detained or imprisoned.

CHAPTER 6

"Let Us Die to Make Men Free"

On April 12, 1861, Confederate batteries ringing Charleston Harbor unleashed a barrage of cannon fire on the Union-held Fort Sumter that lasted for almost 36 hours. The bombardment came after months of ultimatums by the Confederacy for the US government to turn over all military forts and establishments and for all Union troops to withdraw from Confederate territory. The commander of the garrison at Fort Sumter, Major Anderson, refused to bow to the ultimatums, only lowering the American flag after the bombardment ceased. The war had begun.

In response to the attack on Fort Sumter, President Lincoln issued a call for the states to raise volunteer militias to put down the rebellion in the seceding states. Four southern states—Virginia, Tennessee, North Carolina, and Arkansas—refused to fight other Southerners and voted to seceded themselves and join the Confederacy.

Lincoln now found himself, and Washington, in a precarious position. The nation's capital straddled the border of Virginia and Maryland, so Union forces were quickly dispatched to secure the area immediately surrounding the District of Columbia. Maryland posed a particular challenge; as a slave state, Confederate sympathies ran high. Lincoln decided to suspend the **writ of *habeus corpus*** to prevent any attempt on the part of Maryland's citizens to rebel and join the Confederacy, a move decried by many. He also had to tread carefully in the matters of Kentucky and Missouri, slaveholding border states that had chosen to remain with the Union despite high levels of Confederate sympathy.

After the first major engagement at Bull Run ended in a Union defeat, both sides realized the war would not be a short, simple affair. Armies trained and prepared for a fight that, ultimately, would last for four years and claim the lives of an estimated 620,000 to 700,000 men.

Throughout this time, Lincoln began to consider the best avenue to address the issue of slavery without alienating the Border States or those in the free states who believed in preserving the Union but not necessarily the abolition of slavery.

Wherever Union Armies went in the South, thousands of slaves would seek protection behind their lines. Beginning in 1861, the government's policy was not to return these runaway slaves to their owners. These people, known as "contrabands," would live in camps, move with the armies, and provide labor or other useful services to the Union cause.

Dead confederate soldiers on the battlefield at Antietam, where the Union army won a tactical victory in September 1862. Such victories made Lincoln believe the government could take stronger action on slavery. He issued the Emancipation Proclamation a few weeks after the battle.

    Plagued with a series of inept or hesitant generals who consistently lost to the better strategy and battlefield tactics of Confederate generals like Thomas "Stonewall" Jackson and Robert E. Lee, and despite pressure from abolitionists to make the war a crusade for freedom, Lincoln believed he could do nothing about slavery without a solid Union military victory. The Union needed to do four crucial things to win the war: secure control over the Mississippi River, prevent the South from accessing international trade that benefited its war effort, stop the Confederate army, and destroy the South's ability to produce goods and **war materiel**.

    Early military action in Virginia was disastrous for the Union, but armies in the Western Theater that encompassed the Ohio,

A MEASURE TO END THE WAR

The Emancipation Proclamation was not a sweeping measure to abolish slavery across the United States. Though slavery is never explicitly mentioned in the Constitution, certain clauses, such as the Three-Fifths clause, implicitly allowed slavery. It would require a constitutional amendment to change that.

Lincoln recognized the bounds of his constitutional authority, and also knew that he would lose the Border States should he attempt to touch slavery there. He resisted calls to push for emancipation of slaves. In his August 1862 response to abolitionist Horace Greeley, Lincoln asserted that his goal was to save the Union, not end slavery. He wrote, "If I could save the Union without freeing any slave I would do it, and if I could save it by freeing all the slaves I would it; and if I could save it by freeing some and leaving others alone I would also do that. What I do about slavery, and the colored race, I do because I believe it helps to save the Union; and what I forbear, I forbear because I do not believe it would help to save the Union."

But Lincoln also knew that, as Commander in Chief of the armed forces, he had the power to issue executive orders as war measures. The Emancipation Proclamation one such war measure. In states where slavery existed, slaves were seen as property, not people. Because the South relied on slave labor to grow crops and sustain the Confederacy, freeing slaves within the rebellious states would deprive the South of a vital resource. Indeed, once word of the proclamation spread, slaves across the south decided to take their own freedom rather than wait for the Union army to bring it to them.

As more territory came back under Union control and more slaves found their way to freedom, the ability of the Confederacy to maintain its war effort waned, then collapsed.

Cumberland, Tennessee, and Mississippi Rivers fared better. In 1862, General Ulysses S. Grant won a series of victories in the river valleys, and a naval blockade of the entire Confederacy from the Texas border with Mexico to the Union-held ports of eastern Virginia slowly reduced the ability for European trading vessels and smugglers to bring supplies into the Confederacy. Finally, in September 1862, General Lee's Army of Northern Virginia retreated from its attempt to invade the North, after fierce fighting around Antietam Creek in Maryland resulted in a stalemate.

Lincoln seized on the Confederate retreat to claim a tactical victory for the Union, the first major victory in the Eastern Theater of the war. Coupled with Grant's successes in Tennessee and the capture of New Orleans, Lincoln felt the time had come to act on slavery.

"THENCEFORWARD, AND FOREVER FREE"

From the beginning of the war, slaves who found themselves behind Union lines or who managed to escape into Union held territory were considered contraband, and military leaders used laws such as the Confiscation Act to refuse the return of escaped slaves to their owners.

On September 22, 1862, Lincoln issued the Emancipation Proclamation. Effective January 1, 1863, the proclamation freed "all persons held as slaves within any State or designated part of a State, the people whereof shall then be in rebellion against the United States, shall be then, thenceforward, and forever free."

The Emancipation Proclamation was met with mixed reception. Abolitionists cheered its issuance, though noted that it did not go far enough to end slavery everywhere, only in states and regions in rebellion. Lincoln's political opponents believed he had overstepped his bounds, and many Union soldiers themselves were reluctant to fight for the freedom of a people they believed were not equal to them. But regardless of the criticism, the proclamation established that the war was no longer just about

A few months after the Emancipation Proclamation went into effect, the government began recruiting black soldiers. They did not serve in units with white soldiers, although they were commanded by white officers. These members of the 4th US Colored Infantry were assigned to help defend Washington, D.C., in 1864.

the preservation of the Union. It now had a high-reaching moral aspect in the end of the subjugation of African Americans.

FIGHTING FOR THEIR FREEDOM

The Emancipation Proclamation did more than free slaves in Confederate territory. It also authorized the establishment of units of "colored troops," regiments of freed slaves and free blacks to fight for the Union. Almost 200,000 blacks joined the army and navy. Commissioned officers for colored troop units were white, but black soldiers received promotions to non-commissioned officer ranks after demonstrating courage and leadership. Many units distinguished themselves in battle and conduct throughout the second half of the war.

Colored troops faced discrimination even as they joined the fight to free their families held in bondage. The pay for a black soldier was less than that of a white soldier of the same rank; many units also went without proper uniforms or weapons. Additionally, corps commanders were often reluctant to send colored troops into battle, relegating them to menial tasks such as building redoubts and trenchworks. The Confederacy also refused to acknowledge captured black soldiers as prisoners of war, threatening enslavement at best and death at worst for any black soldier caught in battle.

Despite this, black soldiers in the Civil War performed with resilience, dignity, and loyalty. Regiments like the 54th Massachusetts were lauded for their actions in several campaigns in the Carolinas, and a unit of colored troops were the first to walk into the fallen Confederate capital of Richmond, Virginia, in the final days of the war.

Fighting in the army was not the only way blacks contributed to the Union war effort. Blacks served as nurses and orderlies in hospitals, spied for Union commanders, and, in the South, slaves seized opportunities to sabotage the Confederate war effort. The

To learn about the 54th Massachusetts "Glory" Regiment, scan here.

MEN OF COLOR
TO ARMS! TO ARMS!
NOW OR NEVER

This is our golden moment! The Government of the United States calls for every Able-bodied Colored Man to enter the Army for the

Three Years' Service

And join in Fighting the Battles of Liberty and the Union. A new era is open to us. For generations we have [suffered] under the horrors of slavery, outrage and wrong; our manhood has been denied, our citizenship blotted out, or [our souls] seared and burned, our spirits cowed and crushed, and the hopes of the future of our race involved in doubt and [dark]ness. But now our relations to the white race are changed. Now, therefore, is our most precious moment. Let [us rise] to arms!

FAIL NOW, & OUR RACE IS DOOMED

[on] this the soil of our birth. We must now awake, arise, or be forever fallen. If we value liberty, if we wish to be free in this land, if [we love] our country, if we love our families, our children, our home, we must strike *now* while the country calls; we must rise up in the dignity [of our] manhood, and show by our own right arms that we are worthy to be freemen. Our enemies have made the country believe that [we are] craven cowards, without soul, without manhood, without the spirit of soldiers. Shall we die with this stigma resting upon our graves? [Shall] we leave this inheritance of Shame to our Children? No! a thousand times NO! We WILL Rise! The alternative is upon us. Let us [rather] die freemen than live to be slaves. What is life without liberty? We say that we have manhood; now is the time to prove it. A [race of] people that cannot fight may be pitied, but cannot be respected. If we would be regarded *men*, if we would forever silence the [tongue of] Calumny, of Prejudice and Hate, let us Rise Now and Fly to Arms! We have seen what Valor and Heroism our Brothers displayed [at Port] Hudson and Milliken's Bend, though they are just from the galling, poisoning grasp of Slavery, they have startled the World by the most [heroic] heroism. If they have proved themselves heroes, cannot WE PROVE OURSELVES MEN?

ARE FREEMEN LESS BRAVE THAN SLAVES

More than a Million White Men have left Comfortable Homes and joined the Armies of the Union to save their Country. Cannot we leave ours, and swell [the hosts] of the Union, to save our liberties, vindicate our manhood, and deserve well of our Country. MEN OF COLOR! the Englishman, the Irishman, the French[man,] German, the American, have been called to assert their claim to freedom and a manly character, by an appeal to the sword. The day that has seen an en[slaved race] in arms has, in all history, seen their last trial. We now see that our last opportunity has come. If we are not lower in the scale of humanity than E[nglishmen,] Irishmen, White Americans and other Races, we can show it now. Men of Color, Brothers and Fathers, we appeal to you, by all your concern for your[selves and] your liberties, by all your regard for God and humanity, by all your desire for Citizenship and Equality before the law, by all your love for the Country, to [scorn all] subterfuge, listen to nothing that shall deter you from rallying for the Army. Come Forward, and at once Enroll your Names for the Three Years' Service [Strike] now, and you are henceforth and forever Freemen!

E. D. Bassett,	Rev. J. Underdue,	P. J. Armstrong,	Rev. J. C. Gibbs,	Elijah J.
William D. Forten,	John W. Price,	J. W. Simpson,	Daniel George,	John P. B
Frederick Douglass,	Augustus Dorsey,	Rev. J. B. Trusty,	Robert M. Adger,	Robert Jo
Wm. Whipper,	Rev. Stephen Smith,	S. Morgan Smith,	Henry M. Cropper,	O. V. Catt
D. D. Turner,	N. W. Depee,	William E. Gipson,	Rev. J. B. Reeve,	Thos. J. L
Jas. McCrummell,	Dr. J. H. Wilson,	Rev. J. Boulden,	Rev. J. A. Williams,	I. D. Cliff,

An advertisement seeking black Americans to serve in the Union Army, published by Frederick Douglass in 1863.

Underground Railroad also continued to operate through much of the war, until enough territory came under Union control or the Emancipation Proclamation spurred a large enough mass exodus to make enforcement of the fugitive slave law impossible.

THE LEGISLATIVE BATTLE TO ABOLISH SLAVERY

Since the Emancipation Proclamation was a war measure, Republicans in Congress and President Lincoln knew it would not retain its validity once the war ended. A permanent, legislative solution was required if slavery was to end in the United States.

On April 8, 1864, the Republican-controlled Senate passed the Thirteenth Amendment, which states that "neither slavery nor involuntary servitude . . . shall exist within the United States, or any place subject to their jurisdiction." But the battle for its passage in the House continued until January 1865. Lincoln and key Republican members of Congress utilized all their resources to persuade enough Democratic Representatives to either abstain or vote for the amendment's passage by the required two-thirds majority. Still, the amendment would not be enacted unless three-fourths of the states ratified it. Ratification was finally achieved on December 6, 1865.

SURRENDER AND REUNION

Lincoln began formulating a plan to restore Union as early as 1863. His plan called for three parts: a pardon for all Southerners except those who held high-ranking positions in government or the military, that 10 percent of the 1860 voting population swear an oath of allegiance to the United States, and the emancipation of all slaves. A radical faction of the Republican Party, however, wanted harsher terms for the South that would punish the rebels.

To achieve this end, Lincoln met with Alexander Stephens and other representatives from the Confederacy at the Hampton Roads Peace Conference on February 3, 1865. At this meeting, Lincoln outlined his terms for the South's readmission to the Union, as well as secure ratification of the Thirteenth Amendment by the

> **DID YOU KNOW?**
>
> Mississippi did not ratify the Thirteenth Amendment until February 7, 2013, as it failed to submit documentation of its ratification vote. The amendment went into effect without Mississippi's ratification, as the necessary three-fourths of the then 36 states voted in its favor.

Southern states. With a Confederate surrender almost a near certainty by this point, support for the amendment grew in both sections of a war-weary country.

Lincoln did not live to see the ratification of the Thirteenth Amendment. His assassination on April 14, 1865, also dashed the prospects of a speedy restoration of the Union. Radical Republicans called for severe treatment of the South for its rebellion, some acting in revenge for Lincoln's death as well. By the end of 1866, the era of **Reconstruction** gripped the South. With it came new opportunities for freed African Americans.

But so grew resentment and anger among white Southerners who began to cling to a mythology of a "lost cause". Within a decade, many parts of the South were back under the control of those who had hoped to perpetuate slavery in the first place. New regulations and laws came into effect during the advent of the Jim Crow Era that reduced the black population of the South to a state of quasi-slavery and second-class citizenship. It would take almost another full century for blacks to receive the rights they had been promised at the end of the Civil War—and even today, the United States still struggles to reconcile with its past as new iterations of racial inequality bring fresh reminders of the legacy of slavery in America.

TEXT-DEPENDENT QUESTIONS

1. Why did Lincoln wait until after the Battle of Antietam to issue the Emancipation Proclamation?
2. What were two major effects of the Emancipation Proclamation?
3. What were the terms of Lincoln's plan to readmit the seceding states to the Union?

RESEARCH PROJECT

Using your library and the internet, research the wartime contributions of African Americans during the Civil War, including but not limited to spying, sabotage, nursing, or fighting in the army. Choose three individuals and write a 3 to 4 page report detailing their participation in the war and evaluating the importance of their actions and others like them.

SERIES GLOSSARY OF KEY TERMS

antebellum period—refers to the period from 1789, after the United States became an independent nation, until the Civil War began in 1861.

aristocracy—the highest class in a society.

cash crop—a crop, such as cotton or tobacco, that is produced primarily for sale at a market. Cultivation of cash crops was very labor-intensive, and required large numbers of slaves.

chattel slavery—a type of slavery in which the enslaved person becomes the personal property (chattel) of the owner and can be bought, sold, or inherited. The person is a slave for life, and their offspring are also enslaved.

domestic slave trade—the buying, selling, and transportation of enslaved people within a territory or country, such as the United States or the Spanish colonies.

Emancipation Proclamation—a presidential proclamation issued in late 1862 that declared that all African-Americans held as slaves in rebellious states during the Civil War would be considered free by the United States government on January 1, 1863.

indentured servants—a form of servitude in which a person agrees to work in exchange for food and shelter for a certain period of time.

Middle Passage—name for the slave trade route from Africa to America across the Atlantic Ocean, which was infamous due to its horrific conditions.

overseer—a plantation manager who supervised the work activities of slaves.

Quaker—a member of the Religious Society of Friends, a Christian group that was strongly opposed to slavery.

segregation—the separation of people in their daily lives based on race.

sharecropper—a tenant farmer in the South who was given credit by the landowner to pay for seeds, tools, living quarters, and food, in exchange for a share of his crop at the time of harvesting.

tenant farmer—a person who farms on rented land.

transatlantic slave trade—the capturing, enslaving, buying, selling, and transportation of Africans across the Atlantic to the Americas.

Underground Railroad—term for the route used by runaway slaves to reach freedom, either in the Northern states or Canada.

white supremacy—a belief that white people are superior to people of all other races, especially the black race, and should therefore dominate society.

slave codes—laws passed in the South to restrict the activity of slaves. Some laws made it illegal to teach slaves how to read or write. Others prevented slaves from moving freely from place to place without a pass, or from holding religious services without the presence of a white man to monitor their activities.

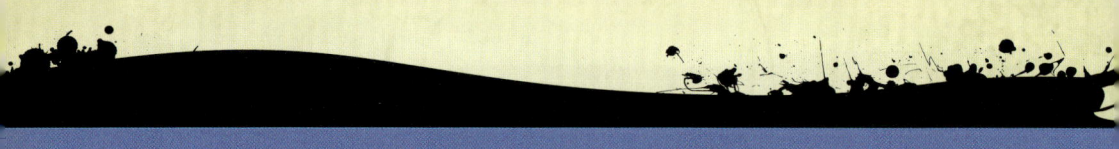

CHAPTER NOTES

p. 7 — "the wolf by the ear ..." Thomas Jefferson to John Holmes, April 22, 1820. Transcript at Library of Congress Manuscript Division (accessed January 5, 2019). https://www.loc.gov/exhibits/jefferson/159.html

p. 10 — "attempts to enslave ..." Thomas Paine, "African Slavery in America," March 8, 1775, *Pennsylvania Journal and the Weekly Advertiser*, reprinted by the Constitution Society (accessed January 7, 2019). https://www.constitution.org/tp/afri.htm

p. 15 — "Representatives and direct Taxes ..." United States Constitution (accessed January 5, 2019). https://www.usconstitution.net/const.pdf

p. 23 — "the several acts and parts ..." South Carolina Ordinance of Nullification, November 24, 1832. Transcript at the Avalon Project, Yale Law School (accessed January 30, 2019). http://avalon.law.yale.edu/19th_century/ordnull.asp

p. 26 — "neither slavery ..." Wilmot Proviso, 1846. Transcript at Blue and Gray Trail (accessed January 31, 2019). http://blueandgraytrail.com/event/Wilmot_Proviso_[full_text]

p. 29 — "overspread the continent ..." John O'Sullivan, "Annexation," *The United States Magazine and Democratic Review*, 1845. Transcript at the American Yawp Reader (accessed February 3, 2019). https://www.americanyawp.com/reader/manifest-destiny/john-osullivan-declares-americas-manifest-destiny-1845/

p. 32 — "to attack slavery in all its forms ..." *The North Star*, 1847-1859. Transcript at the National Museum of African American History and Culture (accessed February 6, 2019). https://nmaahc.si.edu/object/nmaahc_2014.151.3

p. 34 — "all persons born or naturalized ..." Fourteenth Amendment, US Constitution (1868). Transcript at Cornell Law School (accessed February 6, 2019). https://www.law.cornell.edu/constitution/amendmentxiv

p. 33 — "powers not delegated ..." Tenth Amendment, US Constitution (1791). Transcript at Cornell Law School (accessed February

6, 2019). https://www.law.cornell.edu/constitution/tenth_amendment)

p. 45 "the better to protect our persons …" John Brown, Provisional Constitution and Ordinances for the People of the United States, 1858. Transcript at Famous Trials (accessed February 10, 2019). http://www.famous-trials.com/johnbrown/614-browconstitution)

p. 46 "the crimes of this guilty land …" John Brown's Last Speech, October 16, 1859. Transcript at History is a Weapon (accessed February 10, 2019). https://www.historyisaweapon.com/defcon1/johnbrown.html

p. 51 "endure permanently half slave …" Abraham Lincoln, House Divided Speech, June 16, 1858. Transcript at Abraham Lincoln Online (accessed February 13, 2019). http://www.abrahamlincolnonline.org/lincoln/speeches/house.htm

p. 50 "Take care. By this rule …" Abraham Lincoln, fragment on Slavery, July 1, 1854. Transcript at the National Park Service (accessed February 13, 2019). https://www.nps.gov/liho/learn/historyculture/slavery.htm

p. 62 "If I could save the Union …" Abraham Lincoln letter to Horace Greeley, August 22, 1862. Reprinted in Karl Weber, ed., *Lincoln: A President for the Ages* (Washington, D.C.: PublicAffairs Books, 2012), p. 163.

p. 56 "the negro is not …" Alexander Stephens, "Cornerstone Speech," March 21, 1861. Transcript at Teaching American History (accessed February 11, 2019). http://teachingamericanhistory.org/library/document/cornerstone-speech/

p. 63 "all persons held as slaves …" Abraham Lincoln, Emancipation Proclamation, September 22, 1862. Transcript at National Archives Online Exhibits (accessed February 15, 2019). https://www.archives.gov/exhibits/featured-documents/emancipation-proclamation/transcript.html)

p. 67 "neither slavery nor involuntary servitude …" Thirteenth Amendment to US Constitution, 1865.

FURTHER READING

Blight, David W., and Brooks D. Simpson, eds. *Union and Emancipation: Essays on Politics and Race in the Civil War Era.* Kent, OH: Kent State University Press, 2007.

Epperson, James. *Causes of the Civil War.* Stockton, NJ: OTTN Publishing, 2006.

Horwitz, Tony. *Midnight Rising: John Brown and the Raid That Sparked the Civil War.* New York: Henry Hold and Company, LLC, 2011.

Levine, Bruce. *Half Slave and Half Free: The Roots of the Civil War.* New York: Hill & Wang, 2005.

McPherson, James. M. *Battle Cry of Freedom: The Civil War Era.* New York: Oxford University Press, 2003.

———. *The Negro's Civil War: How American Blacks Felt and Acted During the War for the Union.* New York: Vintage Books, 2003.

McPherson, James M., and James K. Hogue. *Ordeal by Fire: The Civil War and Reconstruction.* New York: McGraw-Hill Higher Education, 2009.

Sinha, Manisha. *The Slave's Cause: A History of Abolition.* New Haven, CT: Yale University Press, 2016.

INTERNET RESOURCES

www.pbs.org/kenburns/civil-war

The PBS website dedicated to Ken Burns's documentary series *The Civil War* contains video clips, historical documents, photographs, and facts about the Civil War (Episode 1 focuses on the causes of the war.)

www.history.com/topics/american-civil-war/american-civil-war-history

The History Channel's website provides an overview of the Civil War era, including an overview of the political, social, and economic situation in the United States in the early to mid-1800s and the war itself, with links to videos, images, and other media resources.

www.battlefields.org/learn/articles/trigger-events-civil-war

The American Battlefield Trust offers an overview of the events that triggered the outbreak of the Civil War, with links to articles detailing each major event. The larger American Battlefield Trust's website contains a variety of resources about the Civil War Era.

www.britannica.com/event/American-Civil-War

Brittannica's online encyclopedia entry on the American Civil War gives an extensive overview of the era, with links to other Brittannica.com entries about slavery, the events to be considered among the chief causes of the war, and the war itself.

www.historynet.com/civil-war

HistoryNet provides an extensive collection of resources pertaining to the facts and events of the Civil War, from its causes to its effects. The website includes links to articles about the role of African Americans in the war and the history of slavery in America, as well access to articles from its print publications, *Civil War Magazine* and *America's Civil War*.

CHRONOLOGY

1619 The first African slaves are brought to Virginia.

1787 The Northwest Ordinance prohibits slavery in territories located north of the Ohio River and east of the Mississippi River. The Constitutional Convention agrees on the Three-Fifths Compromise.

1793 The first Fugitive Slave Law enforces a constitutional measure denying trial by jury to a fugitive slave, leaving the individual's fate up to federal or state judges.

1793 Eli Whitney's invention of the cotton gin results in greater profitability of cotton cultivation, leading to the westward spread of slave labor.

1808 Congress passes legislation ending American participation in the Trans-Atlantic Slave Trade; the ban will be inconsistently enforced for the next fifty-three years.

1820 The Missouri Compromise establishes that there shall be no restriction on slavery in Missouri, but that slavery will be prohibited in the Louisiana Territory north of 36°30´ latitude.

1821 Missouri enters the Union as a slave state; the admission of Maine as a free state maintains the balance of free and slave states.

1832 The New England Antislavery Society is organized by white and black abolitionists, including William Lloyd Garrison.

1833 Senators Henry Clay and John Calhoun propose the Compromise Tariff to lower an unpopular 1832 tariff that sparked the Nullification Crisis; Congress adopts the measure.

1836 Congress passes what becomes known as the gag rule, which prevents Congress from discussing abolitionist petitions. The rule is repealed in 1844.

1845 Texas enters the Union as a slave state.

1846 The Mexican War begins; Congress debates the Wilmot Proviso, which would ban slavery in all new territory that could potentially be acquired from Mexico should the US win the war.

1848 The Mexican War ends with an American victory, resulting in the acquisition of new western territory; the Free Soil Party forms to oppose the expansion of slavery into new western territories.

1850 The Compromise of 1850 admits California to the Union as a free state and grants voters in the New Mexico and Utah territories the right to decide whether slavery will be allowed. A new, harsher version of the Fugitive Slave Act makes the federal government responsible for apprehending and returning all escaped slaves.

1854 The Kansas-Nebraska Act repeals the Missouri Compromise, authorizing settlers in the territory to self-determine the status of slavery in their local communities.

1856 Abolitionist John Brown participates in a bloody antislavery uprising in Kansas, killing five proslavery activists himself; the series of bloody attacks and counterattacks throughout the territory leads to the region being nicknamed "Bleeding Kansas."

1857 The Supreme Court rules that banning slavery in the territories is unconstitutional, and that Dred Scott is not a citizen and therefore not afforded the same rights as citizens.

1858 Abraham Lincoln and Stephen Douglas engage in a series of debates, arguing primarily about whether slavery should be brought to an end in all US territories.

1859 John Brown's failed raid on the federal arsenal at Harpers Ferry, Virginia, makes him a martyr to abolitionists and creates panic in the South.

1860 Despite not even being on the ballot in multiple Southern states, Abraham Lincoln wins the presidential election. South Carolina votes to secede from the Union.

1861 The Confederate States of America is formed. In April, Confederate harbor batteries fire on Fort Sumter. Lincoln calls for 75,000 troops to be raised to put down the insurrection.

1863 The Emancipation Proclamation goes into effect on January 1, freeing all slaves in all states and territories not under control of the United States government.

1865 Robert E. Lee's surrender of the Confederate Army on April 9 effectively ends the war. The Thirteenth Amendment, abolishing slavery in the United States forever, is ratified on December 6.

INDEX

abolition, 26, 61
  and Emancipation Proclamation, 61–63
  growth of, 31–33, 46
  moral arguments supporting, 33, 39
  and politics, 32–33
  roots of, 9–10
  See also Underground Railroad
Adams, Abigail, 10
  See also abolition
African Americans
  as "contraband," 60, 63
  and Dred Scott case, 34, 51
  effects of Civil War on, 68
  and fugitive slave laws, 35
  during Jim Crow Era, 68
  lynching of, 38
  and participation in Civil War, 58, 66
  in Union Army, 64
  uprisings by, 45–46
Alabama, 19
American Anti-Slavery Society, 31, 44
American Revolution, 8–9, 31, 35
Articles of Confederation, 6, 12

Battle of Antietam, 61
Battle of Bull Run, 60
Bell, John (senator), 52–54
Bleeding Kansas, 39, 42–43, 49, 76
Bonaparte, Napoleon, 19
Breckinridge, John C. (vice president), 52–54
Brown, John, 43–46, 49, 54, 73, 76
  See also abolition

Calhoun, John C. (senator), 22, 33, 41, 76
California, 39–40, 77
citizenship, 34
Civil War, 58–68, 77

Clay, Henry (senator), 7, 21, 38, 40–41, 76
colonization, 8
Common Sense, 10
Compromise of 1850, 36, 38, 40, 76–77
Confederate States of America, 56, 59–68, 76–77
Constitution, 7, 12, 14, 16, 35
  Article I, 15
  Fourteenth Amendment, 34, 72
  "fugitive slave clause," 35
  Tenth Amendment, 72
  Tenth Amendment to, 33
  Thirteenth Amendment, 50, 67–68, 73
Constitutional Union Party, 52–53
contraband, 60, 63
cotton economy, 29–30
cotton gin, 16, 28–29, 76

Declaration of Independence, 12
Democratic Party, 36, 42
  See also Northern Democrats; Southern Democrats
Douglas, Stephen A. (senator), 40–43, 49, 51–54
Douglass, Frederick, 32, 66
  See also abolition
Dred Scott case, 34, 51, 76–77

Election of 1860, 49–53
Electoral College, 48, 54
Emancipation Proclamation, 50, 61–64, 67, 70, 73, 76
encomienda system, 18, 24
Enlightenment, 9

federalism, 28, 33, 35
Force Bill of 1833, 23
Fort Sumter, 59, 76
Founding Fathers, 10, 12, 16
Fourteenth Amendment, 34, 72
France, 20

Franklin, Benjamin, 10–11
Freeport Doctrine, 51
Free Soil Party, 26, 31, 36, 42–43, 76
Fugitive Slave Act (1793), 35, 76
Fugitive Slave Act (1850), 35–36, 77

Georgia, 9, 15, 18
Grant, Ulysses S., 63
Great Compromise, 14–16
Greeley, Horace, 62
  See also abolition
Guerrero Decree, 24
  See also Mexico

habeus corpus, 58–59
Hampton Roads Peace Conference, 67
Harper's Ferry, 44–46, 49, 54, 76
House Divided speech, 51, 73
House of Representatives, 14–16, 32
Houston, Samuel, 25

Jackson, Andrew, 23–24
Jackson, Thomas "Stonewall," 61
Jefferson, Thomas, 12, 72
Jim Crow Era, 68

Kansas-Nebraska Act, 41–42, 76–77
Kentucky, 13, 19, 60

Lay, Benjamin, 10
  See also abolition
Lee, Robert E., 45, 61, 77
Lincoln, Abraham, 36, 48–51, 53–54, 59–63, 67–68
Louis and Clark Expedition, 20
Louisiana Territory, 19–20
lynching, 38

Maine, 21, 76
Manifest Destiny, 28–29

Massachusetts, 21
Mexican-American War, 24–25, 40, 76
Mexico, 24–26
　See also Guerrero Decree
Middle Passage, 70
Mississippi, 19, 28
Missouri, 20–21, 60
Missouri Compromise, 20–22, 34, 40–41, 76–77

New England Antislavery Society, 76
North Carolina, 15
Northern Democrats, 52–53
　See also Democratic Party
North Star, The, 32, 72
Northwest Ordinance, 13, 19, 76
nullification, 22–24, 33, 56, 76

Ordinance of Nullification, 22–23, 72
Ordinance of Secession, 23
　See also secession

Paine, Thomas, 10, 72
　See also abolition
Pennsylvania Society for Promoting the Abolition of Slavery, 10–11
　See also abolition
Philadelphia, 31
Pierce, Franklin, 42
popular sovereignty, 38, 42, 51

QR Video
　54th Massachusetts Regiment, 65
　Election of 1860, 51
　John Brown and Harper's Ferry, 45
　Missouri Compromise, 21
　overview of American slavery, 8
　slavery and cotton economy, 30
Quakers, 10, 71

See also abolition

Reconstruction, 58, 68
Republican Party, 26, 36, 42, 49, 53, 67
Rush, Benjamin, 10
　See also abolition

Scott, Dred, 34
secession, 23–24, 28, 33, 38, 54, 56, 59
sectionalism, 16, 19–22, 25, 29, 39–40, 49, 53
Senate, 14, 16
slave economy, 9, 13, 16
slavery
　armed uprisings against, 45–46
　attitudes toward, 9–10, 63
　brutal practices in, 8–9
　in colonial America, 7–8, 10, 76
　and Dred Scott case, 42, 51
　early opponents of, 9–10
　early prohibitions on, 13
　economy and, 30, 62
　and Founding Fathers, 10, 12, 16
　and freed slaves, 60, 63
　and fugitive laws, 35–36, 40, 67
　and human rights, 9
　international trade and, 15, 71
　key component of Confederacy, 56
　laws enforcing, 71
　legal challenge to, 34
　Lincoln's struggles with, 50
　in Louisiana Territory, 20
　Manifest Destiny and, 28–29
　moral arguments opposing, 33, 39, 51
　nations that practiced, 8, 20
　and politics, 32–33, 36
　proponents of, 23, 30–31
　and Southern economy, 12–13, 16, 19, 29

　statistics, 8
　in Texas, 25–26
　See also abolition; Emancipation Proclamation
South Carolina, 15, 22, 54–56, 59, 72, 77
Southern Democrats, 52–53
　See also Democratic Party
Spain, 18, 20, 24
states' rights, 33–35, 40, 42
Stephens, Alexander, 56, 67
Supreme Court, 34, 77

Taney, Roger (Chief Justice), 34
Tennessee, 13, 19
Tenth Amendment, 33, 72
Texas, 24–25, 40–41
Thirteenth Amendment, 50, 67–68, 73, 76
Thomas Jefferson, 7
Three-Fifths Compromise, 14–16, 62
Trans-Atlantic Slave Trade, 76

Underground Railroad, 35, 44, 67, 71
　See also abolition
Union Army, 60, 63–66
　4th US Colored Infantry, 64
　54th Massachusetts Regiment, 64
　colored troops, 64

Virginia, 12, 15, 45, 61

Washington, DC, 41, 59
Washington, George, 14
Wheatly Phillis, 10
　See also abolition
Whig Party, 36, 42
Whitney, Eli, 29, 76
　See also cotton gin
Wilmot, David, 25
Wilmot Proviso, 26, 72, 76
women's rights, 32
Woolman, John, 10
　See also abolition

79

AUTHOR'S BIOGRAPHY

Jennifer L. Rowan teaches secondary social studies for Charlotte-Mecklenburg Schools in Charlotte, North Carolina. She holds two master's degrees, including a Master of Science in literacy education, and has over twelve years of teaching experience in New York and North Carolina. She is also a freelance writer and editor, and an author of fiction. A native of upstate New York, near Syracuse, she now lives in the greater Charlotte area with her family.

CREDITS

© Marcorubino | Dreamstime.com: 12; Everett Collection: 11, 16, 28, 40, 44, 46, 64; Independence National Historical Park: 14; Library of Congress: 6, 18, 23, 26, 31, 34, 38, 42, 43, 48, 52, 55, 58, 60, 61, 66; "The Old Flag Never Touched the Ground," a National Guard Heritage Painting by Rick Reeves, courtesy the National Guard Bureau: 1; © OTTN Publishing: 22, 53.